Music

Compiled by
Marlene Peterson

Well-Educated Mother's Heart Learning Library
Libraries of Hope

Music

Music Talks With Children, by Thomas Tapper, Philadelphia: Theodore Presser, (1898).

Young People's History of Music, by James C. Macy, Boston: Oliver Ditson & Co., (1886).

What Can Music Do For You: A Guide for the Uninitiated, by Harriet A. Seymour, New York, Harper & Brothers Publishers, (1920).

Libraries of Hope, Inc.
Appomattox, Virginia 24522

Website www.librariesofhope.com
Email support@librariesofhope.com

Printed in the United States of America

CONTENTS

Music Talks with Children

By Thomas Tapper

Preface

"Dear child! dear girl! that walkest with me here,
If thou appear untouched by solemn thought,
Thy nature is not therefore less divine:
*   *   *   *   *

"God being with thee when we know it not."
—William Wordsworth.

"Teach me to live! No idler let me be,
But in Thy service hand and heart employ."
—Bayard Taylor.

A book of this kind, though addressed to children, must necessarily reach them through an older person. The purpose is to suggest a few of the many aspects which music may have even to the mind of a child. If these chapters, or whatever may be logically suggested by them, be actually used as the basis of simple Talks with children, music may become to them more than drill and study. They should know it as an art, full of beauty and of dignity; full of pure thought and abounding in joy. Music with these characteristics is the true music of the heart. Unless music gives true pleasure to the young it may be doubted if it is wisely studied.

Our failure to present music to the young in a manner that interests and holds them is due not so much to the fact that music is too difficult for children, but because the children themselves are too difficult for us. In our ignorance we often withhold the rightful inheritance. We must not forget that the slower adult mind often meets a class of difficulties which are not recognized by the unprejudiced child. It is not infrequent that with the old fears in us we persist in recreating difficulties.

There should be ever present with the teacher the thought that music must be led out of the individuality, not driven into it.

The teacher's knowledge is not a hammer, it is a light.

While it is suggested that these chapters be used as the subject-matter for talks with the children, they may read verbatim if desired. There is much in the literature of art that would interest children if given to them discriminatingly.

THOMAS TAPPER.

BOSTON, October 30, 1896

What The Face Tells.

"And the light dwelleth with him."—Daniel II: 22.

Once a master said to a child:

"If thou wilt study diligently, learn, and do good unto others, thy face shall be filled with light."

So the child studied busily, learned, and sought how she could do good unto others. And every little while she ran to the glass to see if the light was coming. But at each time she was disappointed. No light was there. Try as faithfully as she would, and look as often as she would, it was always the same.

I do not know if she doubted the master or not; but it is certain she did not know what to make of it. She grieved, and day after day her disappointment grew. At length she could bear it no longer, so she went to the master and said:

"Dear master, I have been so diligent! I have tried to learn and to do good unto others. Yet every time I have sought in my face the light which you promised, it has not been there. No, not a single time."

Now the master listened intently, and watching her face as she spoke, he said:

"Thou poor little one, in this moment, as thou hast spoken to me, thy face has been so filled with light that thou wouldst not believe. And dost thou know why? It is because every word thou hast spoken in this moment has come from thy heart.

"Thou must learn in the first days this lesson: When the thought and the deed are in the heart, then the light is in the face, always, and it is there at no other time. It could not be. And what is in thy heart when thou art before the glass? In that moment hast thou turned away from diligence, and from learning, and from the love of doing good unto others and in thy heart there is left only the poor curiosity to see the light which can never shine when it is sought. Thou canst never see the light of thy own face. For thee that light is forever within, and it will not prosper thy way to want to look upon it. It is only as thou art faithful that this is added unto thee."

Sorrowing yet more than before the little child said:

"Master, I do not understand what thou hast said, yet I believe thee; but the wish is yet within me to see the light of my face, if only for once. Thou who art wise, tell me why it is denied me."

And the master made answer:

"It is denied to us all. No one may see the light of his own face. Therefore thou shalt labor daily with diligence that thy light shall shine before others. And if thou wouldst see the light thou shalt cause it to shine in another. That is the greatest of all—to bring forth the light. And to do this, thou shalt of thyself be faithful in all things. By what thou art thou must show diligence, the love for learning, and the desire to do good unto others, even as these things have been taught thee."

Why We Should Study Music.

"Music makes people more gentle and meek, more modest and understanding."—Martin Luther.

It was this same music lover who said once, "Music is the fairest gift of God." Just these words should be a sufficient answer to the question which we have asked in this Talk, but a little more may make it clearer. Here we are, gathered together to talk about music. We know music is pleasing; to many of us it is even more than a pleasure; of course, it is difficult to get the lessons properly and we must struggle and strive. Often the way seems so rude and stony that we cannot advance. We are hurt, and hot tears of discouragement come, and we sit down dejected feeling it were best never to try again. But even when the tears flow the fastest we feel something within us which makes us listen. We can really hear our thoughts battling to tell us something,—prompted by the heart, we may be sure.

And what is music making our thoughts say?

"Have I not been a pleasure and a comfort to you? Have I not set you to singing and to dancing many and many times? Have I not let you sing your greatest happiness? And am I not ever about you, at home, in school, in church? Even in the streets I have never deserted you. Always, always I have made you merry. But this was music you heard. Now you have said you wished to know me yourself; to have me come to dwell in your heart that you might have me understandingly, and because I ask labor of you for this, you sit here with your hot tears in your eyes and not a bit of me present in your heart. Listen! Am I not there? Yes, just a bit. Now more and more, and now will you give me up because I make you work a little?"

Well, we all have just this experience and we always feel ashamed of our discouragements; but even this does not tell us why we should study music. Some people study it because they have to do so; others because they love it. Surely it must be best with those who out of their hearts choose to learn about tones and the messages they tell.

Did you ever notice how people seem willing to stop any employment if music comes near? Even in the busiest streets of a city the organ-man will make us listen to his tunes. In spite of the hurry and the crowd and the jumble of noises, still the organ-tones go everywhere clear, full, melodious, bidding us heed them. Perhaps we mark the music with the hand, or walk differently, or begin to sing with it. In one way or another the music will make us do something—that shows its power. I have seen in many European towns a group of children about the organ-man, dancing or singing as he played and enjoying every tune to the utmost. This taught me that music of every kind has its lover, and that with a little pains and a little patience the love for music belongs to all alike, and may be increased if other things do not push it aside.

Now, one of the first things to be said of music is that it makes happiness, and what makes happiness is good for us, because happiness not only lightens the heart, but it is one of the best ways to make the light come to the face. The moment we study music we learn a severe lesson, and that is this: There can be no use in our trying to be musicians unless we are willing to learn perfect order in all the music-tasks we do.

In this, music is a particularly severe mistress. Nothing slovenly, untidy, or out of order will do. The count must be absolutely right, not fast nor slow as our fancy dictates, but even and regular. The hands must do their task together in a friendly manner; the one never crowding nor hurrying the other, each willing to yield to the other when the right moment comes. The feet must never use the pedals so as to make the harmonies mingle wrongly, but at just the right moment must make the strings sing together as the composer desires. The thoughts can never for a single moment wander from the playing; they must remain faithful, preparing what is to come and commanding the hands to do exactly the right task in the right way. That shows us, you see, the second quality and a strict one of music. It will not allow us to be disorderly, and more than this, it teaches us a habit for order that will be a gain to us in every other task. Now let us see:

First, we should study music for the happiness it will give us.

Second, we should study music for the order it teaches us.

There is a third reason. If music gives us happiness, do we not in learning it gain a power to contribute happiness to others? That is one of the greatest pleasures in learning. Not only does the knowledge prove of use and joy to us, but we can constantly make it useful and joy-giving to others. Does this not teach us how thankful we should be to all those who live usefully? And think of all the men who have passed their lives writing beautiful thoughts, singing out of their very hearts, day after day, all their life long, for the joy of others forever after.

In our next Talk we shall learn that pure thought, written out of the heart, is forever a good in the world. From this we shall learn that to study music rightly is to cultivate in our own hearts the same good thought which the composer had. Hence the third reason we can find for studying music is that it makes us able to help and to cheer others, to help them by willingly imparting the little knowledge we have, and to cheer them by playing the beautiful thoughts in tone which we have learned.

These are three great reasons, truly, but there are many others. Let us speak about one of them. In some of the Talks we are to have we shall learn that true music comes from a true heart; and that great music—that is the classics—is the thought of men who are pure and noble, learned in the way to write, and anxious never to write anything but the best. There is plainly a great deal of good to us if we study daily the music of men such as these. In this way we are brought in touch with the greatest thought. This constant presence and influence will mold our thoughts to greater strength and greater beauty. When we read the history of music, we shall see that the greatest composers have always been willing to study in their first days the master works of their time. They have strengthened their thoughts by contact with thoughts stronger than their own, and we may gain in just the same way if we will. We know now that there are many reasons why it is good for us to study music. We have spoken particularly of four of these. They are:

First, for the happiness it will give us.

Second, for the order it demands of us.

Third, for the power it gives us to help and cheer others.

Fourth, for the great and pure thought it brings before us and raises in us.

All these things, are they true, you ask? If the little child had asked that of the master he would have said:

"These things shalt thou find real because they make thee brave. And the pain and the drudgery and the hot tears shall be the easier to bear for this knowledge, which should be strong within thee as a pure faith."

Music in the Heart.

"Raffaello's genius goes directly to the heart."
—*Autobiography of Benvenuto Cellini.*

The only true way to learn is by doing. The skill of the hand and the skill of the thought can be brought out only by use. We shall not become very skilful, nor very learned, nor very good unless we daily devote ourselves to tasks— often difficult and unpleasant—which shall bring to us wisdom, or success, or goodness. None of these things, nor any other like them, come merely by talking about them. That is the worst way of all—merely to talk and not to act. But if we talk truthfully and act with care, we shall gain a great deal. Pleasant companionship often brings forth thoughts which if we follow them industriously, lead a long way in a good direction.

I do not know that any one has likened music to a country. But we can make the comparison, and then it becomes plain that we may either wander through it, seeing the beautiful things, wondering about them, and talking over our admiration and our wonder; or we may join to this a true and an earnest inquiry, which shall give us, as a reward, the clear understanding of some things which we see. Let us travel in this way; first, because we shall gain true knowledge by it, but better still, because we shall thereby learn in the first days that the truest pleasures and the dearest happinesses are those for which we have done something; those for which we have given both of labor and of pains.

One of the wisest little philosophers in the world was Polissena, and I think she became wise just because she labored. As we become more and more acquainted with true music we shall learn this: True music is that which is born in some one's heart. "All immortal writers speak out of the heart." Nothing could be truer; and as they speak out of their hearts you may be sure they intend to speak into ours. Nowhere else. As true music is made in some one's heart, we must feel it in our own hearts as we play it or it will mean nothing. The heart must make it warm, then the beauties of the music will come out. It is strange how our moods tell themselves. All we do with our eyes and with our ears, with the tongue and with the hands, what we do with our thoughts even, is sure to say of itself whether we are doing with a willing heart or not. It is curious that the truth will come out of whatever seems to be a secret, but curious as it may be, it does come out. We must think of that.

Every one of us knows the difference between doing willingly and unwillingly. We know that things done with joy and with eagerness are well done and seem to spring directly from the heart. Not only that, but they really inspire joy and eagerness in those who are about us. Inspire is just the word. Look it up in your dictionary and see that it means exactly what happens—to breathe into—they breathe joy and happiness into all things else, and it comes out of our hearts.

Now happiness can be told in many ways: in laughter, in the eyes, in a game, in a life like that of Polissena's, in anything, but in nothing that does not win the heart. As happiness can be shown in anything, it can be shown in music. We can put happiness into play, likewise we can put happiness into music. And as much of it as we put into anything will come out. Besides, we might just as well learn now as at another time, this: Whatever we put into what we do will come out. It may be happiness or idleness or hatred or courage; whatever goes into what we do comes out very plainly. Everything, remember. That means much. If you should practise for an hour, wishing all the time to be doing something else, you may be sure that your wish is coming out of your playing so plainly that everyone knows it. Do you think that is strange? Well, it may be, but it is strictly true.

No one may be able to explain why and how, but certainly it is true that as we play our music all that goes on in the heart finds its way into the head, and the arms, and the hands, into the music, off through the air, and into the hearts of every one who is listening. So it is a valuable truth for us to remember, that whatever we put into our music will come out and we cannot stop it; and other people will get it, and know what we are by it.

Once we fully understand how music will show forth our inmost feelings we shall begin to understand its truthfulness and its power, as well as its beauty. We shall see from our first days that music will tell the truth. That will help us to understand a little the true mission of art, "either to state a true thing, or adorn a serviceable one." The moment we understand this a very little we shall begin to love art. We shall be glad and willing for music to reveal us, to show the spirit within us, because little by little with the understanding will come love and reverence for the beautiful thoughts that are locked up in tones.

Men who want to tell something to very many people, many of whom they do not know and to whom they cannot go, write down all they have to say and make a book of it. There are some men, however, who have many beautiful thoughts which they wish to tell to those who can understand; these may dwell in their own land or in other lands; in their own time or in future time. But the message of these men is so beautiful and so delicate that it cannot be told in words, so they tell it in music. Then, in their own land and in other lands, in their own day and forever after, people can find out the delicate thoughts by studying the pages of the music, seeking with their hearts the thought that came out of the master's heart.

Do you wonder that composers revere their art? We are told of Chopin that art was for him a high and holy vocation. Do you wonder? Let me read you a few words about his devotion: "In order to become a skilful and able master he studied, without dreaming of the... fame he would obtain." "Nothing could be purer, more exalted, than his thoughts," because he knew that if his thoughts were not pure the impurity would come out in his music.

The music that has first been felt in the heart and then written down finds its way and tells all about the heart, where it was born. When you play and feel that you are playing from the heart, you may be sure you are on the right path. The beautiful thing is, that this is true no matter how simple music is. The very simplest will tell all about us. Remember, in playing music that great and good men have put into tones thoughts which will be a joy and comfort to the world forever. Some one of these Talks will be about classic and common music. But even now I am sure we understand that good music comes from pure thought, and pure thought comes from a good heart. That, surely, is clear and simple.

Pure music is earnest and songful. It has meaning in every part. No tone is without a lofty purpose. That is true music. It is classic from the heart that is put into it.

By being faithful to our music it will do for us more than we can dream. Do you know the inscription that used to be over the north gate of the city of Siena, in Italy?

"Siena opens not only her gates, but her heart to you."

The Tones about Us.

"Scientific education ought to teach us to see the invisible as well as the visible in nature."

—*John Tyndall.*

There used to live in England a famous scientist named Tyndall, who was interested, among other things, in the study of sound. He studied sounds of all kinds, made experiments with them, wrote down what he observed, and out of it all he wrote a book, useful to all who desire to learn about sound and its nature.

One day, Tyndall and a friend were walking up one of the mountains of the Alps. As they ascended the path, Tyndall's attention was attracted by a shrill sound, which seemed to come from the ground at his feet. Being a trained thinker he was at once curious to know what was the cause of this. By looking carefully he found that it came from a myriad of small insects which swarmed by the side of the path. Having satisfied himself as to what it was he spoke to his companion about the shrill tone and was surprised to learn that he could not hear it. Tyndall's friend could hear all ordinary sound perfectly well. This, however, seemed to be sound of such a character as did not reach his sense of hearing. One who like Tyndall listened carefully to sounds of all kinds would quickly detect anything uncommon. This little incident teaches us that sounds may go on about us and yet we know nothing of them. Also it teaches us to think about tones, seek them, and in the first days increase our acquaintance and familiarity with them.

Men of science, who study the different ways in which the mind works, tell us that habit and also a busy mind frequently make us unconscious of many things about us. Sometimes we have not noticed the clock strike, although we have been in the room on the hour; or someone speaks to us, and because we are thinking of something else we fail to hear what is said to us. It certainly is true that very many people do not hear half of the sounds that go on about them, sounds which, if but heeded, would teach people a great deal. And of all people, those who study music should be particularly attentive to sounds of all kinds. Indeed, the only way to begin a music education is to begin by learning to listen. Robert Schumann, a German composer, once wrote a set of rules for young musicians. As it was Schumann's habit to write only what was absolutely needed we may be sure he regarded his rules as very important. There are sixty-eight of them, and the very first has reference to taking particular notice of the tones about us. If we learn it from memory we shall understand it better and think of it oftener. Besides that, we shall have memorized the serious thought of a truly good and great man. This is what he says:

"The cultivation of the ear is of the greatest importance. Endeavor early to distinguish each tone and key. Find out the exact tone sounded by the bell, the glass, and the cuckoo."

There is certainly a good hint in this. Let us follow it day by day, and we shall see how many are the tones about us which we scarcely ever notice. We should frequently listen and find who of us can distinguish the greatest number of different sounds. Then we shall learn to listen attentively to sounds and noises. Bit by bit all sounds, especially beautiful ones, will take on a new and deeper meaning to us; they will be full of a previously unrecognized beauty which will teach us to love music more and more sincerely.

In order that we may better understand how sounds are related to each other we should learn early to sing the major scale so that it will go readily up and down as a melody. As we become more and more familiar with it we must think frequently of its separate tones so as to feel just how each one sounds in the scale, how it fits in the scale, and just what it says, in fact; we shall then notice after a while that we can hear the scale with the inner ear, which is finer and more delicate.

We should have names for the scale-tones like the pretty Italian syllables, or, if not these, whatever our teacher suggests. Then we should have a conception of the tones as they are related. We should learn that every tone of the scale is colored by the tonic. Everyone gets a character from the tonic which tells us all about it, because we learn to hear its relation to its principal tone. In a little while, with patience, we shall be able to hear the scale-tones in any order we may choose to think them. That power will be a fine help forever after—we must be sure to get it in the first days.

Whenever we hear two tones we should try to find them on the piano. This will make us listen more attentively to the tone sounded by the clock, the church-bell, the bird, the drinking-glass. And what a lot there are, like the squeaking door, the cricket, the noise of the wind and rain, the puff of the engine, and all the other sounds we hear in a day. Bit by bit, in this way, our familiarity with tones will grow and we shall be well repaid for all the trouble. Gradually we shall become better listeners—but about listening we are to speak in our next Talk. This, however, may be said now: Let us always be sure to listen with special care to two tones, calling one the tonic, or first, of the major scale and finding what degree the other is, or near what degree it lies. This will make us better acquainted with the scale and we shall learn that all the music we have comes out of it.

We must also listen to tones so that we can tell something about them besides their scale names. We must learn to describe tones, tell whether they are high or low, sweet or harsh, loud or soft, long or short. For instance, through the window I can hear a church-bell. Someone is ringing it slowly so that the tones are long. The tone is not a very high one (it is G above middle C) and the quality is rich and mellow. This describes the church-bell tone quite well, and in like manner we may describe all the sounds we hear. We should make it a habit often to stand or to sit perfectly still and to listen to everything that goes on about us. Even in the country, where all seems as quiet as possible, we shall be surprised at the great number of sounds.

There are some other tones to which I fear we are prone not to listen. I mean the tones which the piano makes when we play finger-exercises. We think perhaps of the finger motion, which is not all; or we think of nothing, which is very bad; or our thoughts begin to picture other things even while we play, which is the worst of all, and bit by bit we actually forget what we are doing. One of the quickest ways to become unable to hear sounds correctly is to play the piano without thinking fully of what we are doing. Therefore it must be a rule never to play a tone without listening acutely to it. If in the first days we determine to do this and remain faithful to it, we shall always touch the piano keys carefully, thoughtfully, and reverentially.

Elsewhere we shall have some definite tone lessons for the purpose of making us familiar with the tones about us. But no rule can exceed in importance this one, never to make any music unthinkingly.

By care and practice we soon become so skilful as to notice tones with the readiness we notice colors in the garden. The sense of tone must be as strong in us as is the sense of color. Then we shall be able to tell differences of tones which are nearly the same, as readily as we can now tell two varieties of yellow, for instance. A bit of perseverance in this and the beauties even of common sounds shall be revealed to us.

Listening.

"You must listen as if listening were your life."
—*Phillips Brooks.*

In our last Talk we learned that it was quite possible for sounds to be about us and yet we not hear them. Sometimes, as in the case of Tyndall's companion, it is because we are not capable; at other times, as when the clock strikes and we do not hear, it is because we are occupied with other things. It is from this latter fact—being occupied with other things—that we can learn what listening is. Listening is not being occupied with other things. It is being completely attentive to what we are expected to hear.

The condition of being occupied with other thoughts when we should be listening is known as inattention. To listen with full attention, all other things being entirely absent from the mind, is one form of concentration.

Inattention is a destroyer. It divides our power between two or more things when it should be directed upon a single thing. Concentration gives us greater and greater mind-power. If you will look in the dictionary to find what concentration means (you should be good friends with the dictionary) you will find it is made up of *con* meaning with, and *centrum*, a center, "with a center," or "to come to a center." If you hold a magnifying-glass between your hand and the sun you will find that at a

24

certain distance the sunlight is in a circle. By changing the distance with delicacy you can diminish the circle to almost a point,—you make the light come to a center. When the circle of light is large, no particular effect is noted by the hand. When, however, the circle is as small as it can be made you feel a sensation of warmth which, if continued long enough, will really burn the hand. That small circle is the sunlight in concentration. The rays of sunlight, instead of being scattered, are centered. They burn the hand because they are full of power—powerful.

By way of example: Let the different rays stand for inattention and the tiny circle of light for concentration. The former has little or no power; the latter is full of power. This very well illustrates what happens, both when our thoughts are scattered over a large area, and when they are brought together—concentrated—in a small circle. The first listening indeed which should claim our attention is not tone-listening, but listening to what is said to us. No one under a good teacher ever learns well who is not attentive and obedient. And then listening and doing are inseparably joined. Tone-listening makes us self-critical and observant, and we are assured by men of science that unless we become good observers in our early years, it is later impossible for us.

In the previous Talk we spoke about listening to all kinds of sounds, particularly those out-of-doors. In this Talk we shall speak only of real music-listening. You know, now, that music born out of the heart is the thought of a good man. Of course, beautiful thoughts of any kind should be listened to not only with attention, but with reverence. Reverence is the tribute which the thoughtful listener pays to the music of a man who has expressed himself beautifully in tone. This at once reveals to us that we should listen to what is great for the purpose of getting ideals. We hear what we hope to attain. It is said of the violinist, Pierre Baillot, that when only ten years of age he heard the playing of Viotti, and though he did not hear it again for twenty years the performance ever remained in his mind as an ideal to be realized in his studies, and he worked to attain it.

The pupils of the great Viennese teacher of the piano, Theodor Leschetizky, say he asks no question more frequently than "Can you not hear?" It is not only difficult to listen to ourselves, but listening is one thing and decidedly a superior thing, while hearing is another and equally inferior thing. And it shows us, when we think of it, that no self-criticism is possible until we forget all things else and listen to what we are doing and listen with concentration. It now becomes clear to us that no one becomes an intelligent musician who is not skilled in tone sense, in listening, and having thoughts about what is heard.

We may read again from the excellent rules of Robert Schumann:

"Frequently sing in choruses, especially the middle parts; this will help to make you musical."

Out of this we learn to try to hear more than the melody, to try sometimes not to think of the melody, but to listen only to that which accompanies it. When, in school, you sing in two and three parts, notice how one is inclined always to sing the soprano. The melody pulls us away from another part if we are not concentrated upon our part. Yet notice how beautifully musical the lower parts are. Listen intently to them whatever part you sing.

It seems in music that we learn to listen in two directions. First, by training the attention merely to follow prominent sounds and to be conscious of all of them; then, later, we do not need to think so much of the prominent melody but we strive to hear the accompanying parts. These are the melodies which are somewhat concealed by the principal one; not truly concealed either, for they are plain enough if we will listen. They make one think of flowers hidden in the grass and foliage. They are none the less beautiful though they are concealed; for the sunlight seeks them out and makes them blossom.

We find hidden melodies in all good music because it is the character of good music to have interesting and beautiful melodic thought everywhere. There are never meaningless tones allowed. Every sound says something and is needed. It is curious that in our playing the moment we put our thoughts upon any tone or voice part with the desire to hear it, it comes out at once as plainly as if it was the highest melody. That illustrates the power of thought concentrated upon even a hidden thing. You know how in Bach even the piano works move as if all parts were to be sung by voices. It reminds one of conversation; of the story, of the question and answer, of the merry chat in a pleasant company. Some bits of sentence are tripping and full of laughter, others grave and majestic, others have wonderful dignity of heart and mind.

Such qualities give music interest and meaning in every part. It will not take you long to discover that it is just the absence of these qualities that makes other music common.

The melody is not sustained by anything particularly well worth listening to. One might say that good music is like the foliage of the garden, every leaf and petal variously yet finely formed, and all combined to make a beautiful whole.

When you have learned carefully to follow the accompaniment of a melody, try to follow the single voice parts in the chorus, particularly the Bass, Tenor, and Alto. And when you go to orchestral concerts learn early to follow special instruments like the clarinet, the oboe, the drum.

Especially try to follow the lower strings, the viola, the cello, and the bass. They are strongly characteristic. You will learn their peculiar qualities only by giving them special and concentrated thought. You will now see that acute and careful listening has its definite ways and purposes. Here they are:

I. Listening comes from concentration.

II. When listening to great music it must be with reverence as well as with attention.

III. We must listen for ideals.

IV. We must listen in order to be self-critical.

V. Constant listening to true music reveals that there is never a tone used unless it has a meaning.

And besides all this we must think that among those who listen to us there may be some one who has learned this careful concentrated way. Then we shall have it ever in mind to "play as if in the presence of a master."

Thinking in Tone.

"The gods for labor sell us all good things."
—*Epicharmus.*

Perhaps you have some doubt as to exactly what is meant by music-thinking. Being somewhat acquainted with composers and with music, the thought may here come to you that all the music we hear in the world must have been made by somebody—by many somebodies, in fact. They have had to sit down, and forgetting all things else, listen intently to the music-thought which fills the mind. If you will sit quietly by yourself you will discover that you can easily think words and sentences and really hear them in the mind without pronouncing anything. In quite the same way the composer sits and hears music, tone by tone, and as clearly as if it were played by a piano or an orchestra. And to him the tones have a clear meaning, just as words have a clear meaning to us. Naturally, one can see that there could be no other way. Unless the composer can think out everything exactly there could be no music, for music must be written, and one can only write what one thinks. So at this point the thought to remember is this: Music must exist in some one's mind before others can have it to hear and enjoy.

In like manner—just the same manner, in fact—the painter is one who thinks pictures; the sculptor, one who thinks statues; the architect, one who thinks buildings.

They think these things just as you think words; and as you tell your thoughts in spoken words, so they tell their thoughts in printed music, in painted pictures, in chiseled statues, and in erected buildings. Now, from all this it should be clear to you that there can be nothing which has not first been thought of by someone. You think the door must be closed and you close it; you think you must know the time and you look at the clock; you think the one hand should play more loudly than the other and you try to do it.

Power to get things and to do things comes to us rapidly only in the fairy-tales. In the real, beautiful, healthy world in which we live we have to work hard and honestly for the power either to get things or to do things. By faithful labor must we win what we want. What we do not labor for we do not get. That is a condition of things so simple that a child can readily understand it. But all, children and their elders, are apt to forget it. In the life of every great man there is a story different from that of every other great man, but in every one of them this truth about laboring for the power one has is found.

In our Talk on Listening, it was said that the sounds we hear around us are the more easily understood if we first become familiar with the melody which is called the major scale. But in order to think music it is necessary to know it—in fact, music-thinking is impossible without it. As it is no trouble to learn the scale, all of you should get it fixed in the mind quickly and securely.

It is now possible for you to hear the scale without singing its tones aloud. Listen and see if that is not so! Now think of the melodies you know, the songs you sing, the pieces you play. You can sing them quite loudly (can you sing them?) or in a medium tone, or you can hum them softly as if to yourself; or further yet, you can think them without making the faintest sound, and every tone will be as plain as when you sang it the loudest. Here, I can tell you that Beethoven wrote many of his greatest works when he was so deaf that he could not hear the music he made. Hence, he must have been able to write it out of his thought just as he wanted it to sound. When you understand these steps and ways you will then know about the beginning of music-thinking.

Let us inquire in this Talk what the piano has to do in our music-thinking. What relation is there between the music in the mind and the tones produced by the piano? It seems really as if the piano were a photographic camera, making for us a picture of what we have written,—a camera so subtle indeed, that it pictures not things we can see and touch, but invisible things which exist only within us. But faithful as the piano is in this, it may become the means of doing us much injury. We may get into the habit of trusting the piano to think for us, of making it do so, in fact. Instead of looking carefully through the pages of our new music, reading and understanding it with the mind, we run to the piano and with such playing-skill as we have we sit down and use our hands instead of our minds. Now a great many do that, young and old. But the only people who have a chance to conceive their music rightly are the young; the old, if they have not already learned to do it, never can. That is a law which cannot be changed.

We have talked about listening so much that it should now be a settled habit in us. If it is we are learning every day a little about tones, their qualities and character. And we do this not alone by hearing the tones, but by giving great heed to them. Let us now remember this: listening is not of the ears but of the thoughts. It is thought concentrated upon hearing. The more this habit of tone-listening goes on in us, the more power we shall get out of our ability to read music. All these things help one another. We shall soon begin to discover that we not only have thoughts about sounding-tones, but about printed tones. This comes more as our knowledge of the scale increases.

We can now learn one of the greatest and one of the most wonderful truths of science: Great knowledge of anything comes from never ceasing to study the first steps.

The major scale, as we first learn it, seems a perfectly simple thing. But if we think of it all our lives we shall never discover the wonders there are in it. Hence, three simple rules for us to follow in learning to think music are these:

1. To listen to all tones.

2. Never to stop studying the major scale.

3. To become accustomed to hear tones within.

If we are faithful to these we shall, with increasing study and industry, become more and more independent of the piano. We shall never think with our hands, nor depend upon anything outside of ourselves for the meaning contained in printed tone-thought.

If now we join two things we shall get the strength of both united, which is greater than of either alone.

If in our playing lessons we have only the very purest music (heart music, remember), and if we are faithful in our simpler thinking lessons, we shall gain the power not only of pure thought, but of stronger and stronger thought. This comes of being daily in the presence of great thoughts—for we are in the presence of great thoughts when we study great music, or read a great poem, or look at a great picture, or at a great building. All these things are but signs made manifest,—that is to say, made plain to us—of the pure thought of their makers.

Thomas Carlyle, a Scotch author of this century, spoke very truly when he said:

"Great men are profitable company; we cannot look upon a great man without gaining something by him."

What We See and Hear.

"You must feel the mountains above you while you work upon your little garden."—*Phillips Brooks.*

Somewhere else we shall have some definite lessons in music-thinking. Let us then devote this Talk to finding out what is suggested to us by the things we see and hear.

Once a boy wrote down little songs. When the people asked him how he could do it, he replied by saying that he made his songs from thoughts which most other people let slip. We have already talked about thought and about learning to express it. If a person of pure thought will only store it up and become able to express it properly, when the time comes he can make little songs or many other things; for all things are made of thought. The poem is stored-up thought expressed in words; the great cathedral like the one at Winchester, in England, or the one near the Rhine, at Cologne, in Germany, is stored-up thought expressed in stone. So with the picture and the statue: they are stored-up thought on canvas and in marble. In short, we learn by looking at great things just what the little ones are; and we know from poems and buildings and the like, that these, and even commoner things, like a well-kept garden, a tidy room, a carefully learned lesson, even a smile on one's face result, every one of them, from stored-up thought.

We can consequently make a definition of THINGS by saying they are what is thought. Things are made of thought. Even if you cannot understand this fully now, keep it by you and as you grow older its truth will be more and more clear. It will be luminous. Luminous is just the word, for it comes from a word in another language and means light. Now the better you understand things the more light you have about them. And out of this you can understand how well ignorance has been compared with darkness. Hence, from the poem, the building, the painting, the statue, and from commoner things we can learn, as it was said in a previous Talk, that music is stored-up thought told in beautiful tones.

Now let us heed the valuable part of all this. If poems, statues, and all other beautiful things are made out of stored-up thought (and commoner things are, too), we ought to be able, by studying the things, to tell what kind of a person it was who thought them; or, in other words, who made them. It is true, we can. We can tell all the person's thought, so far as his art and principal work are concerned. Nearly all his life is displayed in the works he makes. We can tell the nature of the man, the amount of study he has done, but best of all we can tell his meaning. The face tells all its past history to one who knows how to look. His intentions are everywhere as plain as can be in what he does.

Thus you see there is more in a person's work than what we see at the first glance. There are reflections in it as plain as those in a mountain lake. And as the mountain lake reflects only what is above it, so the work of the musician, of the artist, of any one in fact, reflects those thoughts which forever hover above the others. Thoughts of good, thoughts of evil, thoughts of generosity, thoughts of selfish vanity, these, and every other kind, are so strongly reflected in the work we do that they are often more plainly seen than the work itself. And with the works of a great artist before us we may find out not only what he did and what he knew, but what he felt and even what he did not want to say.

We now know what music-thinking is. Also, we see why the young musician needs to learn to think music. Really, he is not a musician until he can think correctly in tone. And further than this, when we have some understanding of music-thought we not only think about what we play and hear, but we begin to inquire what story it tells and what meaning it should convey. We begin to seek in music for the thought and intention of the composer, and, little by little, even before we know it, we begin to seek out what kind of mind and heart the composer had. We begin really to study his character from the works he has left us.

We have now taken the first really intelligent step toward knowing for ourselves something about common and classic music. Later on, as our ability increases, this will be of great value to us. We begin to see, bit by bit, what the author intended. That is the real test of it all. We do not want to find mere jingle in music, we want music that says something. Even a very young child knows that "eenty meenty meiny moe" is not real sense, though it is a pleasant string of sounds to say in a game.

Thus we learn to look into what we hear and into what we see and try to find how much thought there is in it, and the kind of thought it is. We want to know if goodness is expressed; if the best work of the man is before us, or if, for a lower reason, his selfishness and vanity are most prominent. And let us remember that as we seek these things in the works of others, so others of thoughtful kind will watch our doings, our playing, our speech, our little habits, and all to see what our intentions are each time we express ourselves. They will look to see what thoughts we are putting into our doings, whether thoughts of goodness or of selfishness. And our actions will always be just as good as the thought we put into them.

Now a great and a common mistake is, that sometimes we hope by some mysterious change, as in a fairy tale, that they will be better than what we intend. But in the first days let us learn that this is not possible.

The Classics.

"Genuine work done faithfully, that is eternal."
—*Thomas Carlyle.*

The older we grow and the more we study, the more we shall hear about the classics, about classic music, and classic art, and classic books. From the beginning let us keep it in our minds that one of our duties is to find out the difference between what is classic and what is not. Then we shall have a proper understanding. An English writer on art says: "The writers and painters of the classic school set down nothing but what is known to be true, and set it down in the perfectest manner possible in their way."

And we have already learned that thought from the heart, expressed in tones, is good music. On the other hand, a thought with the heart not in it, expressed in tone, makes poor or common music. Mendelssohn wrote in one of his letters: "When I have composed a piece just as it springs from my heart, then I have done my duty toward it." But in writing thoughts, whether in words or in tones, there is a very important thing to add to the bidding of the heart. It is the training of the mind. With both of these one works and judges wisely.

With thought and intention ever so pure, but with no education, one would not be able to write for others, and with a little education one would be able to write only in a partially correct way. This brings us to one of the most interesting Talks we shall have. Let us try to make it clear and simple.

We can easily imagine a man both true and good who can neither write nor spell. Happily, in these days, nearly all people who are old enough know how to do both. We can understand that this man may have beautiful thoughts—the thoughts of a true poet or of a true artist—but being unable to write or to spell he could not put his thoughts on paper for others to read and to study. This is the way thoughts are preserved and made into books so that people may benefit by them.

It would, therefore, be necessary for this man, about whom we speak, to get the assistance of someone who knew how to write thoughts and to spell their words. Then, together, they would have to talk about the thoughts, choose proper words, form the sentences, and make all fit rightly together as a writer must who desires to be clear. But it is more than likely that the one who writes would not do all these things to the satisfaction of the other. Of this there could be but one result. The person who had the beautiful thoughts would be forever wishing that he had learned in the first days to write and to spell. Then he could do all these things for himself and show his thoughts to others exactly as he wished them to appear.

Now it is clear that some may have beautiful and valuable thoughts and not know how to write them, while others may have the ability to write without having thoughts worth preserving. Evidently what one must have are both beautiful thoughts and ability to write them.

Did you think when I read you that bit from the letter of Mendelssohn that all a composer has to do is to find in his heart just what he wants to say? As we have already discovered, that is not enough. To show you that Mendelssohn was not afraid of hard work let us read a little from another of his letters. Mendelssohn had resolved to work in Germany and maintain himself. "If I find that I cannot do this, then I must leave it for London or Paris, where it is easier to get on. I see indeed where I should be more honored, and live more gaily and more at my ease than in Germany, where a man must press forward, and toil, and take no rest,—still, if I can succeed there, I prefer the latter."

We can now understand that it is quite the same with word-thinkers and with tone-thinkers. Good thoughts and the proper writing of them make the classics.

Out of this thought there comes another. It is this: Great thoughts, expressed well, out of a great heart, make the works which last the longest; and still further, for one truth leads out of another. Only they can appreciate the classics who have something that is classic within them. They must have the heart true in its feeling, tender in its sentiments. Even a child can have that. They must have the mind trained in the truest and best way of expressing thought. And a child may begin to learn that. Hence we see that a child may be classic worthy. Only we must never, never, no matter what is our ability, think we are better or above others. The more talents one has the more one is expected to do and the greater duty it is.

Thus far we have three truths; now here is a fourth: Some love the classics sooner and better than others because they have more power. And how do they get it? They think more (thought-making); they feel more (heart-learning); and they see more (truth-seeking).

Let us at once go back and gather together these four truths. They are important. Perhaps some of us who are willing to spend the time will learn them from memory.

And to repay us for the trouble of doing it we shall have greater and greater understanding of many things. Here they are:

I. Good thoughts and the proper writing of them make the classics.

II. Great thoughts, expressed well, out of a great heart, make the works which last the longest.

III. Only they can appreciate the classics who have something that is classic within them.

IV. Some love the classics sooner and better than others because they have more power.

What shall these truths teach us? That true music cannot be learned rapidly; that the way of Art is long and difficult. But if the way is long, it is yet beautiful in every turn; if it is difficult, it is yet worth a struggle for what comes. As you read the lives of the great composers you will learn that they went willingly about their tasks, doing each one well. This is done by all great men. Great men take short steps carefully, no matter how rapidly they can go.

One of them wrote: "Success comes with tiny steps." And it comes entirely unsought. Besides all this we are to remember that the power for these things comes from

I. Thought-making;

II. Heart-learning;

III. Truth-seeking.

Now, just to end with let us read a few words from a book I trust we all may read some day: "Great art is the expression of the mind of a great man, and mean art of a weak man." Let us remember that in choosing things to play.

Further on Ruskin says: "If stone work is well put together, it means that a thoughtful man planned it, and a careful man cut it, and an honest man cemented it."

Likewise in these things one can see what is classic— work out of the heart and well done, and that comes from a thoughtful, careful, honest person.

What We Should Play.

"But blessings do not fall in listless hands."
—Bayard Taylor.

We already begin to understand what the classics are. Year by year as our interest in the beautiful increases, we shall gain more definite knowledge about classic art. That which is classic will begin to announce itself in us. Our own choice indicates our taste but does not always indicate what is best for us. And one of the purposes of art is to improve the taste by setting before us the finest works; in these, by study, we find beauty with which we are unacquainted. Thus we enlarge our capacity for it.

Because we are born with taste unformed and untrained you can at once see the reason for gradually increasing the tasks. They are always a little more difficult—like going up a mountain—but they give a finer and finer view. The outlook from the mountain-top cannot be had all at once. We must work our way upward for it. Hence you will observe in your lessons that what was once a fitting task is no longer of quite the same value because of your increased power. But about this especially we shall have a Talk later on.

When one has heard much music of all kinds, one soon begins to understand that there are two kinds commonly chosen. Some players choose true music with pure thought in it, and do their best to play it well after the manner called for by the composer. Their aim is to give truthful expression to the music of a good writer. Other players seem to work from a motive entirely different. They select music which is of a showy character, with much brilliancy and little thought in it. Their aim is not to show what good music is, but to show themselves. The desire of the first is truth, of the second is vanity.

Now, as we examine into this, and into both kinds of music, we discover much. It proves that we must work for the best; for the truthful music, not for the vain music. As we get better acquainted with true music we find it more and more interesting—it keeps saying new things to us. We go to it again and again, getting new meanings. But the showy music soon yields all it has; we find little or nothing more in it than at first. As it was made not from good thought but for display, we cannot find newer and more beautiful thought in it, and the display soon grows tiresome. True music is like the light in a beautifully-cut gem, it seems that we never see all it is—it is never twice the same; always a new radiance comes from it because it is a true gem through and through. It is full of true light, and true light is always opposed to darkness; and darkness is the source of ignorance.

From all this you can now understand the quaintly-expressed opinion of a very wise man, who said: "In discharge of thy place, set before thee the best example." That means whatever we strive to learn should be learned from works of the best kind. In the beginning, we cannot

choose wisely the best examples to set before ourselves;
therefore it is for us to heed what another wise man said:
"As to choice in the study of pieces, ask the advice of more
experienced persons than yourself; by so doing you will
save much time." You thereby save time doubly. Later on
in your life you will have no bad taste to overcome—that
is one saving; and already you know from childhood many
classics, and that is another saving. What we learn in
childhood is a power all our lives.

You can see plainly, now, that both in the choice of
pieces and in the manner of playing them, a person's
character will come out. We saw in the last Talk how
character has to come out in writing. Only a very common
character would select pieces written entirely for a vain
show—of rapid runs, glittering arpeggios, and loud,
unmeaning chords. Worse than that, such a choice of
pieces displays two common people,—three, in fact: A
composer who did not write pure thought from the heart;
a teacher who did not instil good thoughts into the pupil's
heart; and yourself (if really you care for such things) who
play from a vain desire to be considered brilliant.

A player who devotes the mind and the hands only to
what a meaningless composer writes for them is not
worthy of any power. With our hands in music, as with the
tongue in speech, let us strive from the beginning to be
truthful. Let us try in both ways to express the highest
truth we are able to conceive. Then in art we shall, at least,
approach near unto the true artist; and in life we shall

approach near unto the true-life. Every mere empty display-piece we study takes up the time and the opportunity wherein we could learn a good composition, by a master of the heart. And it is only with such music that you will, during your life, get into the hearts of those who are most worthy for you to know. Out of just this thought Schumann has two rules now very easy for us to understand:

"Never help to circulate bad compositions; on the contrary, help to suppress them with earnestness."

"You should neither play bad compositions, nor, unless compelled, listen to them."

We now come to a really definite conclusion about the compositions we should play and to an extent as to how we should play them.

The heart, the mind, and the hands, or the voice, if you sing, should unite in our music; and be consecrated to the beautiful. Consecrate is just exactly the word. Look for it in your dictionary. It comes from two other words, does it not? *Con* meaning with and *sacer* meaning holiness. Thus devote heart and head and hands with holiness to the beautiful. This is very clear, I am sure.

It is also worth doing. "With holiness" describes how to play and really what to play. A composition which has been born of a true man is in thought already consecrated. He has heard it and felt it within himself. Daily you must get closer and closer to these messages and meanings. And are they not already more luminous to you? And do you remember what we said luminous means?

The Lesson.

"All people value most what has cost them much labor."—
Aristotle.

It is true that music is beautiful and that it gives us happiness and comfort. But, nevertheless, music is hard to learn for every one; harder for some than for others, but hard for all. It is well and best that it should be so. We appreciate most highly that which we labor for earnestly. Just imagine if everyone could sing or play merely by wishing it! Then music would be so common and so much the talent of all that it would cease to give us joy. Why? Because one gained it by a wish. That is not enough. From this can we learn to understand the great secret of it all? I think we can. Let us see! The secret is this: Music is a joy because it takes us out of ourselves and we work hard to get it. Music teaches us what a wonderful power there is within us, if we will only strive to bring it out. Education is good for us for this same reason. As you learn more and more about words, you will see more in this word Education.

It means to lead out what is within us. To lead music out of the heart becomes the object, then, of your lessons. One cannot drive music into you; it must be led out.

Where shall we look for music that it may be led out? Only in the heart. That is where all is in every one of us. But often in our hearts there is so much else, so much vanity, self-love, conceit, love for other things, that the music is almost beyond reach. Almost, but never entirely. In the heart of every one is music. But often it is deep, deep down, covered by these other things. The older we grow and the more other things we see and think about, the deeper and deeper down does the music get.

It is like heaping rocks, and dirt, and sticks on a bubbling spring. The spring is down there, bubbling freely beneath it all, still striving to be as free and as songful as before; but it cannot. People may come and go, may pass near to it, and hear not one of its sounds; they may never suspect that there is such a thing ready to go on merrily if it could.

When is the best time to lead water out of the spring, and music out of the heart? Before other things begin to cover it. With music the best time is in the early days, in childhood time—in the first days. We shall hear those words many times. Then little by little the bubbling spring of melody gains its independence; then, even if other things do come in, they cannot bury the music out of sight. The spring has been led forth and has grown stronger.

Thoughtful people who have suffered in learning—all people suffer in learning, thoughtful ones the most— wonder how they can make the task less painful for others. It will always cause us sorrow as well as joy to learn, and many people spend their lives in trying to have as little sorrow as possible come with the learning of the young. When such people are true and good and thoughtful and have infinite kindness, they are teachers; and the teachers impose tasks upon us severely, perhaps, but with kind severity. They study us and music, and they seek out the work each one of us must perform in order that we may keep the heart-springs pure and uncovered. Further than this, they find the way by which we shall lead the waters of life which flow out of the heart-springs. They find the way whither they should flow best.

Often in the doing of these things we find the lessons hard and wearisome, infinitely hard to bear, difficult, and not attractive. We wonder why all these things should be so, and we learn in the moment we ask that question that these painful tasks are the price we are paying for the development of our talent. That is truly the purpose of a lesson. And the dear teacher, wise because she has been painfully over the road herself, knows how good and necessary it is for us to labor as she directs.

Let us suppose you play the piano. There will be two kinds of lessons—one will be for the fingers, one for the mind. But really the mind also guides the finger-work; and the heart must be in all. Your exercises will give you greater power to speak with the fingers. Every new finger-exercise in piano-playing is like a new word in language. Provided with it, you can say more than you could before. The work for the mind is the classics. These are compositions by the greater and lesser masters with which you form the taste, while the technical exercises are provided to give you the power, the ability, to play them. Thus you see how well these two things go together.

Year after year, if you go on patiently, you will add to each of these tasks; more power will come to the fingers and to the mind. All this time you will be coming nearer and nearer to the true music. More and more will be coming out of your heart. The spring will not only continue to bubble clearly but it will become more powerful. Nothing is so wonderful as that.

Do you know what a sad thing it was for the man not to increase that one talent which had been given to him? Perchance you have also one. Then find it, love it, increase it. Know that every step of the way, every bit of task, every moment of faith is paid for in later years ten thousand fold.

If now we remember our Talk on Listening it will serve us. Did we not say then that the first duty of a listener is to the one who speaks for his good? Lesson time is an opportunity above nearly all others when we should listen with love in our attention. Yes, nothing less than that, because—how many times we have heard it already— putting love into anything, is putting the heart into it, and with less than that we do not get all we may have.

This Talk, then, is important, because it gathers together many things that have gone before, and hints at some to come. Let us give the last words to speaking about that. A lesson suggests listening; listening suggests the teacher, who with infinite kindness and severity guides us;

and the teacher suggests the beautiful road along which we go and what we hear as we travel, that is the music of the heart; and the music of the heart has in it the tones about us, and the greater and lesser masters who thought them into beautiful forms. The masters are as servants unto whom there is given to some one talent, to others two, and four, and more, but to each according to his worth, to be guided and employed in truth and honor; increased by each in accordance to his strength.

The Light on the Path.

"Let us seek service and be helpers of one another."

"Master," said the little child, "I am unhappy. Though I have companions and games, they do not content me. Even the music which I love above all the rest is not truly in my heart; nor is it the pleasure to me which it should be. What am I to do?"

And the master replied:

"There is a task, the greatest and severest of all. But a child must learn it. Thou must know from the first days, that all thou doest and sayest, whither thou goest, what thou seekest; these, all these, come from within. All that is seen of thee is of thy inner life. All thy doings, thy goings and comings, thy ways and thy desires, these are from within. And when all these things are for thyself there is misery.

"Now there are many things which may not be had by directly seeking them; of these the greatest are two. The one is that which already has given thee sadness in the heart,—the Light of the Face. And the other is happiness.

"But there is a way in which these are to be found. Dost thou not know that often, even with much trouble, thou canst not please thyself? But always, with little trouble or none, thou canst please another.

"And the way is Service.

"Thou poor little one! Thou hast come with thy complaint of unhappiness; and yet thou hast all that is bright and rare; companions, and music, and a dear home. Dost thou know that there are in the world uncounted poor ones, children like thyself, who have not their daily bread? And yet there are many of them who never fail to say: 'Lead us not into temptation.' And they say this without having tasted of the daily bread for which they have been taught to pray.

"And thou? Thou art unhappy. And thy daily bread is set before thee with music and with sunshine.

"Yet there are little ones, like thyself, who are hungry in the darkness.

"And thou? Thou art unhappy."

The Greater Masters.

"In spite of all, I have never interrupted the study of music."—
Palestrina.

An opera writer of Italy, named Giovanni Pacini, once said that to study the writings of Mozart, Haydn, and Beethoven "lightens the mind of a student, since the classics are a continuous development of the most beautiful and simple melodies," and we sometimes hear it said that great men are they who dare to be simple. In our Talks thus far we have learned one important fact, which is, that music is truth expressed out of the heart. Of course we know that to be in the heart it must be felt, and to be expressed we must know a great deal about writing. Now we are able to imagine quite well what a great master is in music. As Pacini says, his melodies will be simple and beautiful, and as we ourselves know, his simple melodies will be an expression of truth out of the heart.

But to go only as far as this would not be enough. Many can write simply and well, and truthfully, yet not as a master. There must be something else. When we have found out what that something else is we shall understand the masters better and honor them more.

Everywhere in the history of music we read of what men have been willing to do for the love of their art. It is not that they have been willing to do when told; but that they have cheerfully done painful, laborious tasks of their own accord. The name of every master will recall great labor willingly given for music and equally great suffering willingly endured, nay, even sought out, that the music might be purer to them. Poor Palestrina went along many years through life with the scantiest means. But, as he says, "in spite of all, I have never interrupted the study of music." Bach was as simple and loyal a citizen as any land could have, and from the early years when he was a fatherless boy to the days of his sad affliction, he sacrificed always. Think of the miles he walked to hear Buxterhude, the organist; and in the earlier years, when he lived with Johann Christopher, his brother, how eagerly he sought learning in the art that so fascinated him. It was a constant willingness to learn honestly that distinguished him.

Any of us who will labor faithfully with the talents we have can do a great deal—more than we would believe. Even Bach himself said to a pupil: "If thou art equally diligent thou wilt succeed as I have." He recognized that it matters little how much we wish for things to be as we want them; unless our wish-thoughts are forced into prompt action we cannot succeed; for while all thoughts seek action, wish-thoughts demand the most labor.

It would be pleasant to have a Talk about every one of the great masters to see in what particular way each of them sacrificed for the art he loved. In all of them the true qualities come out: in one as earnestness; in another as determination; in another as patriotism; but all are loyal to the art itself. It must be a very plain lesson to us to see that when men are willing to give all their thoughts to a subject they get much from it. And is it not quite as plain to see that no one can get much if he gives but a few unwilling minutes to it? I trust none who hear these Talks will ever think that with a little time given to their music, and that not freely given, they can ever get either pleasure or comfort from it. They never can. And rather than do it so they would better leave it undone. If we set out on the way to go to the masters we shall get there only by earnestness. Lagging is a disgrace to the one who travels and to the one to whom we go. It shows his laziness on the one hand, and his misunderstanding of the master on the other; for if he understood he would take no listless step.

Now we have said again and again that true music comes from the heart, and is simple. At the same time we find it difficult to understand the music of the masters. That is, some of us find it so. It seems anything but simple to us; and naturally we conclude that there is something wrong somewhere. We sit at our tasks, poring over the music, and we grow discouraged because we cannot play it. To think it a very hard task is natural, and we cannot bear to hear such tones. Well, let us not get discouraged for that; let us see!

First of all, the playing is more difficult to do than the music is to understand. Once a great master of the piano played to a lady who had never heard a great master before, and the playing was like beautiful lace. When it was over and the master had gone away, some one asked the lady how he had played, and she said:

"He played so that the music sounded as I thought it should."

And they asked her what she meant.

"Always I have been taught," she said, "to listen to music and to think it. I have been taught this more than I have been taught to play. And the music of the master-composers I always think of as beautiful and simple but hard to make it sound as it should. Often I have heard others say that the music of the masters is dull, and not beautiful, but that is really not what the people feel. It is difficult for them to play the music rightly. And again they cannot understand this: that art is often simple in, its truth, while those who look upon it are not! simple-hearted, as they regard it. This is hard to understand, but it is the true reason."

Now, if we think of what this cultured lady said, we shall think her wise. Whatever stumbling we may do with our fingers, let us still keep in our minds the purity of the music itself. This will in a sense teach us to regard reverentially the men who, from early years, have added beauties to art for us to enjoy to-day. The wisest of the Greeks said:

"The treasures of the wise men of old, which they have left written in books, I turn over and peruse in company with my friends, and if we find anything good in them, we remark it, and think it a great gain, if we thus become more attracted to one another."

Once an English lady wrote about a verse-writer: "No poet ever clothed so few ideas in so many words." Just opposite to this is a true poet, he who clothes in few words many and noble ideas. A master tells his message in close-set language.

Now, in the last minutes, let us see what a great master is:

I. He will be one who tells a beautiful message simply.

II. He has been willing to sacrifice and suffer for his art.

III. He has lived his every day in the simple desire to know his own heart better.

IV. Always he has concentrated his message into as few tones as possible, and his music, therefore, becomes filled to overflowing with meaning.

About the meaning of the masters, one of them has written this: "Whenever you open the music of Bach, Mozart, or Beethoven, its meaning comes forth to you in a thousand different ways." That is because thousands of different messages from the heart have been concentrated in it.

The Lesser Masters.

"And the soul of a child came into him again."
—*I Kings, XVII: 22.*

If, one day, someone should say to you, earnestly: "Well day are to you!" you would scarcely know what to make of it. You would at once understand that the person had knowledge of words but could not put them together rightly. And if the person continued to talk to you in this manner you might feel inclined to lose your patience and not listen. But if you would stop and consider things and examine yourself you would learn something well worth thinking about.

You would discover that your own ability to put words in the right order has come from being obedient. First of all, you have been willing to imitate what others said until you have thereby learned to speak quite well. Besides that, you have been corrected many times by those about you at home, and in school, until language is at length a careful habit in you. Everyone knows at once what you mean. You see, therefore, that you may combine words in such a manner that you will be easily comprehended by others; or, as in the case of the imaginary person we began with, they may be combined in a perfectly senseless way. Consequently, it is not enough to know words alone, we must know what to do with them. The true art of using words is to put full and clear meaning into a few of them;

to say as much as possible with as few words as you may select.

Tones may be treated in the same manner as words. One can write tones in such a manner as to say quite as senseless a thing as "Well day are to you!" Many do. This teaches you that true and simple tone-sentences, like similar word-sentences, must have for their object to say the fullest and clearest meaning in as little space as possible.

For many hundreds of years thoughtful composers have studied about this. They have tried in every way to discover the secrets underlying tone-writing so that the utmost meaning should come out when they are united. Tones thus arranged according to the laws of music-writing make sense. To learn this art all great composers have studied untiringly. They have recognized the difficulty of putting much meaning in little space, and to gain this ability they have found no labor to be too severe.

We must remember that there is no end of music in the world which was not written by the few men whom we usually call the great composers. Perhaps you will be interested to know about these works. Many of them are really good—your favorite pieces, no doubt. When we think of it, it is with composers as with trees of the forest. Great and small, strong and weak, grow together for the many purposes for which they are created. They could not all be either great or small. There must be many kinds; then the young in time take the place of the old, and the strong survive the weak. Together beneath the same sky, deep-rooted in the beautiful, bountiful earth, they grow side by side. The same sun shines upon them all, the same wind and the same rain come to them, selecting no one before another. What are they all doing? Each living its true life, as best it can. It is true they may not come and go, they may not choose, but as we see them, beautiful in their leaves and branches we feel the good purpose to which they live and, unconsciously, perhaps, we love them.

Among us it is quite the same. Some are more skillful than others. But be our skill great or small, we are not truly using it until we have devoted it to a worthy purpose. And as with us, so it is with the musicians. There are the great and small. The great ones—leaders of thought—we call the great masters. The lesser are earnest men, who have not as much power as the masters, but they are faithful in small things.

They sing lesser songs it is true, but not less beautiful ones. Often these lesser ones think more as we do. They think simply and about the things which we have often in our minds. It is such thoughts as these which we have in our best moments that we love so much when we see them well expressed by one who is a good and delicate writer, either of tones or words. Particularly do we understand these thoughts welling the first years of our music when nearly all the works of the greater composers are above us.

Thus are the many composers (who yet are not great masters) of value to us because they write well a kind of thought which is pure and full of meaning, and which we can understand. They give us true pleasure day after day in the beginning and seem at the same time to help us onward to the ability of understanding the great masters. This they do by giving our thought training in the right direction.

Now, we know that the very best music for a young musician to learn in the first days is that of the lesser tone masters, together with those simpler pieces of the great composers which come within his power to comprehend—within the power of a child's hands and voice. Let us see, once again, if it is not clear:

True composers, great and small, sing from the heart. If one having a little skill turn it unworthily away from the good and true work he might do, then he does not use rightly his one talent. He does not give us true thought in tone. He writes for vanity or a low purpose, and is not a lesser master but he is untrue.

It is not our right to play anything. We may rightly play only that which is full of such good thought as we in our power may understand. It is to supply us with just this that the lesser masters write. In simple, yet clear and beautiful pictures, they tell us many and many a secret of the world of tone into which we shall someday be welcomed by the greater ones if we are faithful unto the lesser.

Harmony and Counterpoint.

"Whilst I was in Florence, I did my utmost to learn the exquisite manner of Michaelangelo, and never once lost sight of it."—*Benvenuto Cellini.*

On any important music subject Schumann has something to say. So with this:

"Learn betimes the fundamental principles of harmony." "Do not be afraid of the words theory, thorough-bass, and the like, they will meet you as friends if you will meet them so."

We now begin to feel how definitely these rules treat everything. They pick out the important subjects and tell the simplest truth about them. The meaning of these two rules is this: From the beginning we must try to understand the grammar of music. Some of the great composers could in childhood write down music with the greatest fluency. Handel, even as a boy, wrote a new church composition for every Sunday. Mozart began to write music when less than five years old, and when he was yet a boy, in Rome, he wrote down a composition, sung by the choir of the Sistine Chapel, which was forbidden to the public.

Harmony and counterpoint stand to music very much as spelling and grammar stand to language. They are the fundamentals of good writing and of good—that is, of correct—thinking in music. Harmony is the art of putting tones together so as correctly to make chords. Counterpoint has to do with composing and joining together simple melodies. A modern writer on counterpoint has said: "The essence of true counterpoint lies in the equal interest which should belong to every part." By examining a few pieces of good counterpoint you will readily see just what this means. The composer has not tried to get merely a correct chord succession, such as we find in a choral. Let us play a choral; any good one of a German master will do. We notice that the soprano is the principal part, and that the other voices, while somewhat melodic, tend rather to support and follow the melody than to be independent. If, now, we play a piece of counterpoint like the G-Minor Prelude by Bach, we shall have quite a good piece of counterpoint, as far as separate melodies being combined is concerned. Let us play the voice-parts separately. We shall find equal melodic interest in each. The chords grow out of the music. Comparing this with the choral, the main difference between harmony and counterpoint should be clear to us. We shall observe that the three voices do not proceed in the same way. If one part moves quickly, as in the bass of the first two measures, the other parts are quieter; if the bass ceases to move rapidly some other voice will take up the motion, as we see in the third and following measures. As a general thing no two voices in contrapuntal writing move in the same way, each voice-part being contrasted with different note-values. This gives greater interest and makes each voice stand forth independently.

At first contrapuntal music may not seem interesting to us. If that is so, it is because we are not in the least degree conscious of the wonderful interest which has been put into every part. The truth is, that in the beginning we cannot fully understand the thought that has been put into the music, but by perseverance it will come to us little by little. This is what makes great music lasting. It is so deftly made, yet so delicately, that we have to go patiently in search of it. We must remember that gems have to be cut and polished from a bit of rock.

In this case the gem is the rich mind-picture which comes to us if we faithfully seek the under-thought. And the seeking is polishing the gem.

Music written entirely by the rules of counterpoint is called contrapuntal music; that written otherwise is known as free harmonic music. In the one case the composer desired to have a beautiful weaving of the parts—clear as the lines in a line-engraving. In the other, the intention is to get effects from tones united into chords, such as is obtained from masses of color in a painting. Neither form may be said to be the superior of the other. Each is valuable in its place, and each has possibilities peculiarly its own, which the other could not give. Pure counterpoint could not give us such a charming effect as Chopin obtains in the first study of Opus 10; nor could the plainer and more free harmonic style give us such delicate bits of tracery as Bach has in his fugues.

If now you will take the trouble to learn two long words, later in your study of music they will be of use to you. The first is Polyphonic; the other is Monophonic. Both, like many other words in our language, are made up of two shorter words, and come from another language— Greek. In both we have "phonic," evidently meaning the same in each case, limited or modified by the preceding part—*poly* and *mono. Phonic* is the Anglicized Greek for sound. We use it in the English word telephonic. Now if we define mono and poly we shall understand these two long words.

Mono means one, poly means many. We say monotone, meaning one tone; also polygon, meaning many sides.

In the musical reference monophonic music means music of one voice, rather than of one tone, and polyphonic music is that for many voices. Simple melodies with or without accompanying chords are monophonic; many melodies woven together, as in the Bach piece which we have looked over, are polyphonic.

In the history of music two men surpassed all others in what they accomplished in counterpoint—that is, in polyphonic writing. The one was Palestrina, an Italian; the other was Bach, a German. Palestrina lived at a time when the music of the church was very poor, so poor, indeed, that the clergy could no longer endure it. Palestrina, however, devoted himself earnestly to composing music strictly adapted to the church use. The parts were all melodic, and woven together with such great skill that they yet remain masterpieces of contrapuntal writing. Later Bach developed counterpoint very much more in the modern way. He did with polyphony for the piano and organ much the same as Palestrina did for the voice. There have never lived greater masters than these in the art of polyphonic music.

There is still another form of writing which is neither strictly harmonic, nor strictly contrapuntal,—it is a combination of both. There is not the plain unadorned harmonic progress as in the simple choral, nor is there the strict voice progression as in the works of Bach. This form of writing which partakes of the beauties of both the others has been called the free harmonic style. It has been followed by all the great masters since the time of Bach, even before, indeed. If you can imagine a beautiful song-melody with an artistic accompaniment, so arranged that all can be played upon the piano, you will understand what the third style is. It is wonderfully free, surely; sometimes proceeding in full free chords, as in the opening measures of the B flat Sonata of Beethoven, again running away from all freedom back to the old style, until the picture looks as old as a monkish costume among modern dress.

All of the great sonatas and symphonies are of this wonderfully varied form of writing. How full it can be of expressiveness you know from the Songs without Words by Mendelssohn, and the Nocturnes of Chopin; how full of flickering humor you hear in the Scherzo of a Beethoven symphony; how full of deep solemnity and grief one feels in the funeral marches.

This school of composition has been followed by both the greater and the lesser masters. Every part is made to say something as naturally and interestingly as possible, being neither too restricted nor too free. Then, in playing, both hands must be equally intelligent, for each has an important part assigned to it.

The great good of study in harmony and counterpoint is that it increases one's appreciation. As soon as we begin to understand the spirit of good writing we begin to play better, because we see more. We begin, perhaps in a small way, to become real music-thinkers. By all these means we learn to understand better and better what the meaning of true writing is. It will be clear to us that a composer is one who thinks pure thoughts in tone, and not one who is a weaver of deceits.

Music and Reading.

"Truly it has been said, a loving heart is the beginning of all knowledge."—Thomas Carlyle.

A beautiful thing in life is the friendship for books. Everyone who loves books pays someday a tribute to them, expressing thankfulness for the joy and comfort they have given. There are in them, for everybody who will seek, wise words, good counsel, companies of great people, fairies, friends for every day, besides wonders we never see nor dream of in daily life.

Some of the great men have told us about their love for books; how they have saved penny by penny slowly to buy one, or how after the day's labor a good book and the firelight were prized above anything else. All tell us how much they owe to books and what a blessing books are. Imagine the number of heart-thoughts there must be in a shelfful of good books! Thoughts in tones or thoughts in words may be of the heart or not. But it is only when they are of the heart that they are worthy of our time.

You will not only love books, but gain from them something of the thoughts they contain. We might, had we time, talk of classic books, but as we have already talked of classic music we know what the principal thing is. It is that good thought, out of the heart, be expressed in a scholarly way—"Great thought needs great expression." This teaches us the necessity for choosing good books for our instruction and for our entertainment. They present beautiful pictures to us truthfully, or they present truth to us beautifully. And these are the first test of a written thought—its truth and its beauty.

If you read good books you will have in every volume you get something well worth owning. You should bestow upon it as much care as you would want any other good friend to receive. And if it has contributed help or pleasure to you it is surely worth an abiding place. A fine pleasure will come from a good book even after we are quite done with it. As we see it in years after it has been read there comes back to one a remembrance of all the old pleasures, and with it a sense of thankfulness for so pleasant a friendship. Hence any book that has given us joy or peace or comfort is well worth not only good care, but a place for always; as a worthy bit of property.

In the early days of your music study, it will be a pleasure to you to know that there are many and delightful books about music written, sometimes by music-lovers, sometimes by the composers. The written word-thoughts of the composers are often full of great interest. They not only reveal to us many secrets of the tone-art, but teach us much about the kinds of things and of thoughts which lived in the minds of the composers. We learn definitely not only the music-interests of the composers, but the life-interest as well. It really seems as if we were looking into their houses, seeing the way they lived and worked, and listening to their words. Never afterward do we regard the great names in music as uninteresting. The most charming and attractive pictures cluster about them and it all gives us a new inspiration to be true to music, loyal to the truth of music, and willing to do as we see others have done, and to learn by doing. The lesson we get from the life of every man is, that he must do if he would learn.

I am sure you will spend many delightful minutes with the Letters of a great composer. Everyone is like a talk with the writer. They are so friendly, and so full of the heart, and yet so filled with the man himself. Especially the Letters of Mendelssohn and Schumann will please you. In truth the Letters of all the composers are among the most valuable music writings we have. In some way they seem to explain the music itself: and the composer at once becomes a close friend. But besides these read the biographies. Then it is as if we were personally invited home to the composer and shown all his ways and his life. And besides these, there are some friendly books full of the very best advice as to making us thoughtful musicians; many and many again are the writers who have so loved art—not the art of tone alone, but all other arts as well— that they have told us of it in good and earnest books which are friendly, because they are written from the right place; and that you must know by this time is the heart.

You will soon see when you have read about the composers that true music comes out of true life. Then you will begin to love true life, to be useful, and to help others. But all these things do not come at once. Yet, as we go along step by step, we learn that art is unselfish, and we must be so to enjoy it; art is truthful—we must be so to express it; art is full of life—we must know and live truth in order to appreciate it. And the study of pure thoughts in music, in books, and in our own life will help to all this.

The Hands.

"The skill of their hands still lingers."
—*John Ruskin.*

In one of our Talks, speaking about the thoughts in our hearts, we said that they crept from the heart into our arms and hands, into the music we play, and off to those who hear us, causing in them the thoughts by which they judge us. Thus we see, that as Janus stands sentinel at the doorway of the year, so the hands stand between the secret world of thought within and the questioning world of curiosity without.

If we were not in such a hurry usually, we might stop to think that every one, all over the world, is training the hands for some purpose. And such a variety of purposes! One strives to get skill with tools, another is a conjurer, another spends his life among beautiful and delicate plants, another reads with his fingers. In any one of these or of the countless other ways that the hands may be used, no one may truly be said to have skill until delicacy has been gained. Even in a forcible use of the hands there must be the greatest delicacy in the guidance. You can readily see that when the hands are working at the command of the heart they must be ever ready to make evident the meaning of the heart, and that is expressed in truthful delicacy. Not only are all the people in the world training their hands, but they are, as we have already said, training them in countless different ways.

Have you ever stopped to think of another matter: that all things about us, except the things that live, have been made by hands? And of the things that live very many are cared for by the hands. These thoughts will suggest something to us. Those things which are good and beautiful suggest noble use of the hands; while those which are of no service, harmful and destructive, show an ignoble use. But noble and ignoble use of the hands is only another evidence of thought. Thought that is pure in the heart guides the hands to beautiful ends. And if the heart is impure in its thoughts, of course you know what follows.

I have always been impressed in reading the books of John Ruskin to note how many times he speaks about the hands. Very truly, indeed, does he recognize that back of all hand work there is heart-thought, commanding, directing, actually building. It shows everywhere. The building of a wall with the stones rightly placed demands honor. The builder may be rude, but if his hands place the stones faithfully one upon another, there is surely honor in his heart. If it were not so his hands could not work faithfully.

If the work is finer, like that work in gold which many have learned eagerly in former times, in Rome and Florence, still the spirit must be the same. So we see, that be the work coarse or fine, it is in either case prompted by the same kind of heart-thought.

Many times in these Talks I have spoken of Ruskin's words to you; for two reasons: first, his words are always full of meaning, because he was so full of thought when he wrote them; and second, I would have you, from the first days, know something of him and elect him to your friendship. Many times he will speak to you in short, rude words, impatiently too, but never mind that, his heart is warm and full of good.

Now from what was said a moment ago about the stone work and the gold work we can understand these words:

"No distinction exists between artist and artisan, except that of higher genius or better conduct."

Learn from this then, be the work of our hands what it may, its first quality and the first things for which it shall be judged are its honor, its faithfulness, and its sincerity.

Of themselves the hands are absolutely without power. They cannot move, they cannot do good things nor bad things, they can do nothing until we command them. And how shall this be done? Surely I can understand it if you have wearied of this Talk a little. But I have said all the things just for the sake of answering this question, so that you should understand it. How do we command? not the hands alone but all we do and say?

By our THOUGHTS.

Without them there is no power whatever. Until they have commanded, the hands cannot make a motion; the feet must have direction ordered to them, the tongue must be bidden to speak, and without the command there is nothing.

Of course, all these Talks are about thoughts. But we shall need a little time to speak of them particularly. And little by little it will be clear to us all why the hands need to act thoughtfully. Now the harm of the world is done by two forces,—by evil thought and by thoughtlessness. Then it is no wonder that Ruskin speaks much about the hands, for it is thought that gives them guidance. Can you wonder, that when he says, "the idle and loud of tongue" he associates the "useless hand." These things go together, and together they come either from evil thought or from lack of thought. The moment Ruskin speaks of one who uses his hands with honor, his words glow. So he speaks of the laborer, describing him as "silent, serviceable, honorable, keeping faith, untouched by change, to his country and to Heaven."

Thus, when we are earnestly asked to do something worthy with the hands every day, we can understand why. I do not mean one worthy thing, but some one particular worthy act, especially thought out by us. To do that daily with forethought will purify the heart. It will teach us to devote the hands to that which is worthy. Then another old truth that everyone knows will be clear to us: "As a man—or a child, for that matter—thinketh in his heart, so he is."

Bit by bit the thoughts of this Talk will become clear to you. You will feel more friendly toward them. Then you will really begin to think about hands; your own hands and everybody's hands. You will become truthful of hand, guiding your own thoughtfully; watching those of others carefully. And you will find that in the smallest tasks of your hands you can put forethought, while every use to which people put their hands will teach you something if you observe carefully. It may be folding a paper or picking up a pin, or anything else quite common; that matters not, common things, like any others, can be done rightly.

By this observation we shall see hands performing all sorts of odd tricks. The fingers are drumming, twitching, twirling, closing, opening, and doing a multitude of motions which mean what? Nothing, do you say? Oh! no, indeed; not nothing but something. Fingers and hands which perform all these unnecessary motions are not being commanded by the thoughts, and are acting as a result of no thought; that is, of thoughtlessness. Everyone does it do you say? No, that is not true. Many do these things, but those who command their thoughts never allow it. If we never moved the hands except in a task when we commanded them, we should soon become hand-skilled. The useless movements I have spoken of unskill the hand. They are undoing motions, and teach us that we must govern ourselves if we would become anything. Do you know how it is that people do great things? They command themselves. Having determined to do something, they work and work and work to finish it at any cost. That gives strength and character.

Having observed the hands and their duties, we can readily see the kind of task they must do in music. It is just the same kind of task as laying a wall of stone. Every motion must be done honorably. Everything must be thought out in the mind and heart before the hands are called upon to act. Wise people always go about their tasks this way. Unwise people try the other way, of acting first and thinking it out afterward, and, of course, they always fail. You can now understand that a great pianist is one who has great thought with which to command the hands. And to be sure they will obey his commands at once, he has made them obey him continuously for years. This teaching the hands to obey is called Practice.

The Italian artist, Giotto, once said:

"You may judge my master hood of craft by seeing that I can draw a circle unerringly."

What the Roman Lady Said.

"You may always be successful if you do but set out well, and let good thoughts and practice proceed upon right method."—Marcus Aurelius.

The same wise Roman emperor who said this tells us a very pretty thing about his mother, which shows us what a wise lady she must have been, and how in the days of his manhood, with the cares of a great nation upon him, he yet pondered upon the childhood teaching of home. First, he speaks of his grandfather Verus, who, by his example, taught him not to be prone to anger; then of his father, the Emperor Antoninus Pius, from whom he learned to be modest and manly; then of his mother, whose name was Domitia Calvilla. Let us read some of his own words about her, dwelling particularly upon a few of them. He writes: "As for my mother, she taught me to have regard for religion, to be generous and open-handed, and not only to forbear from doing anybody an ill turn, but not so much as to endure the thought of it."

Now these words are the more wonderful when we remember that they were not taken down by a scribe in the pleasant apartments of the royal palace in Rome, but were written by the Emperor himself on the battlefield; for this part of his famous book is signed: "Written in the country of the Quadi."

In our last Talk on the Hands we came to the conclusion, that unless the hands were commanded they could not act. And on inquiring as to what gave these commands we found it was the thoughts. Many people believe it is perfectly safe to think anything, to have even evil thoughts in their hearts, for thoughts being hidden, they say, cannot be seen by others. But a strange thing about thought is this: The moment we have a thought, good or bad, it strives to get out of us and become an action. And it most always succeeds. Not at once, perhaps, for thoughts like seeds will often slumber a long time before they spring into life. So it becomes very clear to us that if we wish to be on the alert we must not watch our actions, but look within and guard the thoughts; for they are the springs of action.

You now see, I am sure, how wise the Emperor's mother was in teaching her boy not even to endure a thought to do evil unto others. For the thought would get stronger and stronger, and suddenly become an action. Certainly; and hence the first thing to learn in this Talk is just these words:

Thoughts become actions.

That is an important thing. In a short time you will see, that if you do not learn it you can never enjoy music, nor beautiful things, nor the days themselves. Let us see how this will come about.

I have told your teacher the name of the book which was written by the Roman lady's boy. Well, in that book, running through it like a golden thread, is this bit of teaching from his mother.

Not only did he think of it and write it on the battlefield, but at all times there seemed to come to him more and more wisdom from it. And he tells us this same thought over and over again in different words. Sometimes it leads him to say very droll things; for instance:

"Have you any sense in your head? Yes. Why do you not make use of it then? For if this does its part, for what more can you wish?" Then, a very good thought which we frequently hear:

"Your manners will very much depend upon what you frequently think." There are many others, but these show us that the meaning of his mother's words went deep, teaching that not action must be guarded but the thought which gives rise to action. Now, what can be the value of speaking about the Roman lady? Let us see.

In music, the tones are made either by the hands or by the voice. And to make a tone is to do something. This doing something is an action, and action comes from thought. No music, then, can be made unless it be made by thinking. And the right playing of good music must come from the right thinking of good thoughts. It may be that you will hear someone say that to think good thoughts is not needed in making good music. Never believe it! Bad thought never made anything good, and never will because it never can. In the very first days you must learn, that good things of all kinds come from good thoughts, because they can come from nothing else.

Here, then, is the second truth of this Talk:

Good music being the fruit of good thought can be played rightly only by one who thinks good thoughts.

This leads us to another matter. First, let us see if everything is clear. True music is written out of good thought; hence, when we begin to study music we are really becoming pupils of good thought. We are learning the thoughts good men have had, trying to feel their truth and meaning, and from them learning to have our own thoughts not only good but constantly better and better. This now seems simple and necessary. We see that if we would faithfully study a composer's work it must be our principal aim to get into his heart. Then everything will be clear to us.

But we can never find our way to the heart of another until we have first found our way somewhere else. Where, do you think? To our own hearts, being willing to be severe with ourselves; not to be deceitful in our own eyes; not to guard the outer act, but the inner thought; not to study nor to be what seems, but what is. This may seem a long and roundabout way of learning to play music, but it is the honest, straightforward way of going to the great masters whom we wish to know.

In one of the books of the Greek general, Xenophon, Socrates is made to say that men do nothing without fire; and quite in the same way we may learn nothing of each other, especially of those greater than ourselves, without thought; which should be pure, strong, inquiring, and kind. With this we may do all.

Thus far we have two principles. Let us review them:

I. Thoughts become actions.

II. Good music being the fruit of good thought can be played rightly only by one who thinks good thoughts.

Now, is it not clear that this can come about only when we watch over our own thoughts and govern them as if they were the thoughts of others? And when we do not so much as endure the thought of harm or evil or wrong we shall be living in the spirit of the Roman lady whose son's life was lived as his mother taught.

The Glory of the Day.

"Be not anxious about to-morrow. Do to-day's duty, fight today's temptation; and do not weaken and disturb yourself by looking forward to things which you cannot see, and could not understand if you saw them."—Charles Kingsley.

Nearly all of us have heard about the little child who one day planted seeds and kept constantly digging them up afterward to see if they were growing. No doubt the child learned that a seed needs not only ground and care, but time. When it is put in the earth it begins to feel its place and to get at home; then, if all is quite right,—but not otherwise—it sends out a tiny rootlet as if it would say that it trusts and believes the earth will feed that rootlet. And if the earth is kind the root grows and finds a solid foothold. At the same time there is another thing happening. When the seed finds it can trust itself to root it feels no longer afraid to show itself. It goes down, down quietly for a firmer hold, and upward feeling the desire for light.

A firm hold and more light, we cannot think too much of what they mean.

Every day that the seed pushes its tender leaves and stem upward it has more and more to encounter. The rains beat it down; the winds bend it to the very earth from which it came; leaves and weeds bury it beneath their strength and abundance, but despite all these things, in the face of death itself, the brave little plant strongly keeps its place. It grows in the face of danger. But how? Day after day, as it fights its way in the air and sunshine, blest or bruised as it may be, the little plant never fails to keep at one thing. That is, to get a firmer and firmer hold. From that it never lets go. Break its leaves and its stem, crush it as you will, stop its upward growth even, but as long as there is a spark of life in it there will be more roots made. It aims from the first moment of its life to get hold strongly.

And it seems as if the plant has always a great motive. The moment it feels it has grasped the mother-earth securely with its roots it turns its strength to making something beautiful. In the air and light, in the dark earth even, every part of the plant is seeking for the means to do a wonderful thing. It drinks in the sunshine, and with the warmth of it, and to the glory of its own life, it blossoms. It has come from a tiny helpless seed to a living plantlet with the smallest stem and root, and while the stem fights for a place in the air the root never ceases to get a strong hold of the dear earth in which the plant finds its home. Then when the home is firmly secured and the days have made the plant stronger and more shapely, it forgets all the rude winds and rain and the drifting leaves, and shows how joyful it is to live by giving something.

Then it is clear that every hardship had its purpose. The rains beat it down, but at the same time they were feeding it; the leaves dropped about and covered it, but that protected its tenderness: and thus in all the trials it finds a blessing. Its growth is stronger, and thankful for all its life it seeks to express this thankfulness. In its heart there is something it is sure. And true enough, out it comes some day in a flower with its color and tenderness and perfume; all from the earth, but taken from it by love which the plant feels for the ground as its home.

We can see from this that the beauty of a plant or of a tree is a sign of its relation to the earth in which it lives. If its hold is weak—if it loosely finds a place for a weak root—it lies on the ground, helpless, strengthless, joyless. But firmly placed and feeling safe in its security, it gives freely of its blossoms; or, year after year, like a tree, shows us its wonderous mass of leaf, all of it a sign that earth and tree are truely united.

It has been said, and no doubt it is true, that one who cares for plants and loves them becomes patient. The plant does not hurry; its growth is slow and often does not show itself; and one who cares for them learns their way of being and of doing. The whole lesson is that of allowing time, and by using it wisely to save it. The true glory of a day for a plant is the air and sunlight and earth-food which it has taken, from which it has become stronger. And every day, one by one, as it proves, contributes something to its strength.

All men who have been patient students of the earth's ways have learned to be careful, to love nature, and to take time. And we all must learn to take time. It is not by careless use that we gain anything, but by putting heart and mind into what must be done. When heart and mind enter our work they affect time curiously; because of the great interest we take in what we do time is not thought of; and what is not thought of, is not noticed.

Hence, the value of time comes to this: to use any time we may have, much or little, with the heart in the task. When that is done there is not only better work accomplished but there are no regrets lingering about to make us feel uncomfortable.

A practice hour can only be an hour of unwelcome labor when one thinks so of it. If we go to the piano with interest in the playing we shall be unconscious of time. Many men who love their labor tell of sitting for hours at their work not knowing that hours have gone by.

If there is a love for music in any of us it will grow as a seed. And as the seed needs the dear mother-earth, so the music needs the heart. When it has taken root there and becomes firmer and firmer it will begin to show itself outwardly as the light of the face. After it is strong and can bear up against what assails it—not the wind and the rain and the dry leaves, but discouragement and hard correction and painful hot tears—then with that strength it will flourish.

Now, sometimes, in the days of its strength the music will seek far more in its life, just as the plant seeks for more and blossoms. The flower in the music is as great for all as for one. It is joy and helpfulness. When for the love of music one seeks to do good then music has borne its blossom.

Thus, by learning the life of a simple plant we learn the true mission of the beautiful art of tone. It must put forth deeply its roots into the heart that it may be fed. It must strive for strength as it grows against whatever may befall it. It must use its food of the heart and its strength for a pure purpose, and there is but one—to give joy.

This turns our thoughts to two things: First, to the men and women who by their usefulness and labor increased the meaning of music. This is the glory of their days. Second, we look to ourselves with feeble hands and perhaps little talent, and the thought comes to us, that with all we have we are to seek not our own glorification but the joy of others.

The Ideal.

"Le beau est aussi utile que l'utile, plus peutêtre."
—*Victor Hugo.*

Mozart once had a friend named Gottfried von Jacquin, who was a man of careful thought, and evidently a good musician,—for we are told that a melody composed by him is frequently said, even to this day, to be by Mozart. This Gottfried lived in Vienna with his father, and to their house Mozart often went. At this time Mozart had an album in which his friends were invited to write. Among the verses is a sentiment written by Gottfried von Jacquin, saying:

"True genius is impossible without heart; no amount of intellect alone or of imagination, no, nor of both together, can make genius. Love is the soul of genius."

Here we have the same truth told us which we have already found for ourselves, namely, that all good music comes from the heart. We have found it by studying music and striving faithfully to get deep into its real meaning. But to-day we have the words of one who was enabled to watch closely as a friend one of the greatest composers that ever lived. And being much with him, hearing the music of the master played by the master himself, put the thought into his head, that it is impossible to be a true genius without heart and love.

From this we shall have courage to know that what we pursue in music is real; that the beauties of great music, though they may just now be beyond us, are true, and exist to those who are prepared for them. When in our struggle to be more capable in art than we are to-day we think of the beauty around us, and desire to be worthy of it, we are then forming an ideal, and ideals are only of value when we strive to live up to them.

Once in Rome there lived a Greek slave—some day you may read his name. He has told us that "if thou wouldst have aught of good, have it from thyself." Of course we see in this, immediately, the truth that has been spoken of in nearly every one of these Talks. It is this: We must, day by day, become better acquainted with ourselves, study our thoughts, have purity of heart, and work for something.

Now, working for something may be accomplished in a simple manner without thinking of it. If every task is done in our best way it adds something to us. It is true and beautiful, too, that the reward for patient, faithful work comes silently to us, and often we do not know of its presence. But some day, finding ourselves stronger, we look to know the cause of it, and we see that the faithfulness of past days has aided us.

So art teaches us a very practical lesson in the beginning. If we would have her favors we must do her labors. If we say to music: "I should love to know you;" music says to us, "Very well, work and your wish shall be gratified." But without that labor we cannot have that wish. The Greek slave knew that and said:

"Thou art unjust, if thou desire to gain those things for nothing."

Now we begin to see that art has no gifts to bestow upon us for nothing. Many think it has, and pursue it until the truth dawns upon them; then, because of their error, they dislike it. To recognize the truth about art and to pursue that truth, despite the hard road, is to have courage. And the Ideal is nothing else than the constant presence of this truth.

And what do we gain by pursuing it? Not common pleasure, but true happiness; not uncertainty, but true understanding; not selfish life, but true and full life. And we can see the beauty of art in nothing more plainly than in the fact that all these things may come to a child, and a new and brighter life is made possible by them.

The very first day we came together, the little child said to the master:

"Master, I do not understand what thou hast said, yet I believe thee."

It is hard, sometimes, to feel the truth and to keep it with us; hard, not only for a child, but for any one; and yet, if with faith we will labor with it until the light comes, then we are truly rewarded and made richer according to our faith.

We must not forget in the first days, as we leave our music, that the path we have taken since we came together is the hardest; not for always, but for now. The right path is hard at first—the wrong one is hard always.

We will understand it all better in other days if we remain faithful now. If, however, we should forget for a moment that art demands our loyalty, there will be no joy or peace in it for us. Worse, perhaps, than starting out upon the wrong path, is the deserting of the right one. Sometimes out of impatience we do this; out of impatience and self-love, which is the worst of all. "Truth is the beginning of all good, and the greatest of all evils is self-love."

With the trials that music costs us, with its pains and discouragements, we might easily doubt all these promises which are contained in our ideals, but we shall be forever saved from deserting them if we remember that these ideals have been persistently held by great men. They have never given them up. One of the strongest characteristics of Bach and of Beethoven was their determination to honor their thoughts. Sometimes we find the same persistence and faithfulness in lesser men.

I am sure you will see this faith beautifully lived in the few facts we have about the life of Johann Christian Kittel, a pupil of Bach, and it is strongly brought out by the pretty story told of him, that when pleased with a pupil's work he would draw aside a curtain which covered a portrait of Bach and let the faithful one gaze upon it for a moment.

That was to him the greatest reward he could give for faithfulness in the music task.

And this reminds us of how the teacher, Pistocchi, who, in teaching the voice, kept in mind a pure tone, a quiet manner of singing, and the true artistic way of doing. Among his pupils was a certain Antonio Bernacchi, who, after leaving his master, began to display his voice by runs and trills and meaningless tones. And this he did, not because of true art, for that was not it, but because it brought him the applause of unthinking people.

Once, when the master, Pistocchi, heard him do this he is said to have exclaimed: "Ah, I taught thee how to sing, and now thou wilt play;" meaning that the true song was gone and the pupil no longer sang out of the heart, but merely out of the throat. Pistocchi kept his ideal pure.

We have then among our ideals two of first importance. The ideal perception of music, as being the true heart-expression of great men; and the ideal of our doings, which is the true heart-expression of ourselves. And to keep these ideals is difficult in two ways: The difficulty of keeping the pure intention of great men ever before us, and the difficulty of keeping close and faithful to the tasks assigned us. Then we can say with the little child:

"Master, I do not understand what thou hast said, yet I believe thee."

The One Talent.

"Then he which had received the one talent came."—
Matthew, XXV: 24.

Someday, when you read about the great composers, you will be delighted with the pictures of their home-life. You will see how they employed music every day. In all cases, as we study them, we learn how very much they have sacrificed for the music they love, studying it daily because of the joy which it yields them. We see them as little children, eager to be taught, wanting to listen to music, and to hear about it. Many of the composers whose child-life is thus interesting were children in very poor families, where things were neither fine nor beautiful, where the necessary things of life were not plentiful, and where all had to be careful and saving so that every bit should be made to go as far as possible. The eagerness and determination of some children in music-history is really wonderful. It is the true determination. And you are not surprised, in following it, to note that it leads the children who have it into lives of great usefulness.

All through the life of Handel we find determination running like a golden thread. He was just as determined to be a musician as Lincoln was to get an education when he read books by the firelight. Handel's father was a surgeon, and knew so little about music that he failed entirely to understand the child. He not only forbade the boy to study music, but even kept him away from school that he might not by any chance learn to read the notes. But one who was in future years to befriend homeless children and to write wondrous music for all the world could not be held back by such devices. By some means, and with friendly assistance (perhaps his mother's), he succeeded in smuggling into the garret a spinet, which is a kind of piano. By placing cloth upon the strings he so deadened the wires that no one downstairs could hear the tones when the spinet was played. And day after day this little lad would sit alone in his garret, learning more and more about the wonders which his heart and his head told him were in the tiny half-dumb spinet before him. Not the more cheerful rooms down-stairs nor the games of his playmates drew him away from the music he loved, the music which he felt in his heart, remember.

One would expect such determination to show itself in many ways. It did. Handel does not disappoint us in this. All through his life he had strong purposes and a strong will—concentration—which led him forward. You know how he followed his father's coach once. Perhaps it was disobedience,—but what a fine thing happened when he reached the duke's palace and played the organ. From that day everyone knew that his life would be devoted to music. Sometimes at home, sometimes in foreign lands, he was always working, thinking, and learning. He is said, in his boyhood, to have copied large quantities of music, and to have composed something every week. This copying made him better acquainted with other music, and the early habit of composition made it easy for him to write his thoughts in after years. Indeed, so skilled did he become, that he wrote one opera—"Rinaldo"—in fourteen days, and the "Messiah" was written in twenty-four days.

Yet parts of his great works he wrote and rewrote until they were exactly as they should be. It will do is a thought that never comes into the head of a great artist. How do you imagine such a man was to his friends? We are told that, "he was in character at once great and simple." And again it has been said that, "his smile was like heaven."

We have seen Handel as the great composer, but he was not so busy in this that his thoughts were not also dwelling upon other things. If ever you go to London, you should of a Sunday morning hear the service at the Foundling Hospital. You will see there many hundreds of boys and girls grouped about the organ. Their singing will seem beautiful to you, from its sweetness and from the simple faith in which it is done. After the service you may go to the many rooms of this home for so many otherwise homeless ones.

There are for you to visit: the playroom, the schoolroom, the long halls with the pretty white cots, and the pleasant dining-room. Here it will please you to see the little ones march into dinner, with their similar dresses, and all looking as happy as possible. But the picture you will, no doubt, longest keep, is that of the children about the organ.

They will tell you there that it was Handel who gave this organ to the chapel, and who, for the benefit of the children who might come here, gave concerts, playing and conducting, which were so successful that they had to be repeated. A "fair copy" of the "Messiah" will be shown you as one of the precious possessions.

It will very plainly be present in your mind how the little boy sat alone playing day after day in the garret, wishing no better pastime than to express the feelings of his heart in tones. Perhaps you will think of his words: "Learn (of) all there is to learn, then choose your own path." He will appeal to you as having possessed an "early completeness of character," which abided always with him. It is evident in following the life of Handel, and it would be equally plain with any other composer, that great talent is developed out of a small beginning, and if small, is yet earnest and determined. From the first days of a great man's life to the last we find constant effort. "I consider those live best who study best to become as good as possible." Music helps us to keep the upper windows open; that is why it does so much for us even if we have but one talent.

To develop our one talent is a duty, just as it is a duty to develop two or five talents. It is given to us to increase. And no one knows how much joy may come to us and to others from the growing of that talent. We gain much in power to give pleasure to others, if the talent we have be made stronger by faithful effort. As we have seen good come forth from the story of the man with many talents, we can see how, similarly, he with one talent has also great power with which he may add unto himself and others.

In all of our Talks it has been evident from what we have said, that music is a beautiful art to us, even though we may have but little of it. But equally we have learned, that for ever so little we must prove ourselves worthy. We must honestly give something for all we get. This is the law, and the purpose of all our Talks is to learn it.

We have, likewise, learned that true music, out of the heart, may not at the first please us, but within it there is a great deal and we must seek it. The history of all who have faithfully studied the works of the great masters is, that for all the thought and time one spends in studying master works a great gain comes. On the other hand, everybody's experience with common music is, that while it may please much at first and even captivate us, yet it soon tires us so that we can scarcely listen patiently to it.

Still a further lesson is, that working with many talents or with one is the same. Talents, one or many, are for increase and faithful development. Handel's life was a determined struggle to make the most of his power. It should be ours.

Love for the Beautiful.

"Every color, every variety of form, has some purpose and explanation."—Sir John Lubbock.

Now, when we are almost at the end of the way we have traveled together, it will be natural to look back upon the road over which we have come. Not all of it will be visible, to be sure. We have forgotten this pleasant scene and that; others, however, remain freshen our minds. And as the days pass and we think over our way there will now and again come to us a scene, a remembrance, so full of beauty and of pleasure that we shall feel rich in the possession of it.

To me there is nothing we have learned together greater in value, richer in truth and comfort than the thought that the beautiful in music and in art is at the same time the good. Even if a person is not at all times good, there is raised in him the feeling of it whenever he consciously looks upon a beautiful object. We see in this how wise it is for one to choose to have beautiful things, to surround others with them, to love them, and to place reverent hands upon them.

We can never make a mistake about gentle hands. Once a lady said to a boy:

"You should touch all things with the same delicacy that one should bestow upon a tender flower. It shows that deep within yourself you are at rest, that you make your hands go forward to a task carefully and with much thought. In the roughest games you play do not forget this; then your hands shall be filled with all the thought you have within yourself."

Sometimes, when I am in a great gallery, the thought is very strong in me, that many (ever, and ever so many) people, in all countries and in all times, have so loved the beautiful as to devote their lives to it. Painters, who have made pictures to delight men for generations, looked and looked and prayed to find the beautiful. And we must believe that one looks out of the heart to find the beautiful or he finds only the common. And the sculptors who have loved marble for the delight they have in beautiful forms, they, too, with eyes seeking beauty, and hands so gentle upon the marble that it almost breathes for them, they, too, have loved the beautiful.

But commoner ones have the tenderest love for what is sweet and fair in life,—people who are neither painters nor sculptors. In their little way—but it is a true way— they have sunlight in their hearts, and with it love for something.

Perhaps it is a flower. I have been told of a man—in fact I have seen him—who could do the cruelest things; who was so bad that he could not be permitted to go free among others, and yet he loved plants so much that if they were put near him he would move quietly among them, touching this one and that; gazing at them, and acting as if he were in another world. As we said once before about the spring, so we may say here about love for the beautiful: it may be covered up with everything that is able to keep it down, but it is always there.

It is always pleasanter to hear about people and their ways than to heed advice. But people and their ways often set us good examples; and we were curious, indeed, if we did not look sharply at ourselves to see just what we are. From all we have been told about the beautiful we can at least learn this: that it sweetens life; that it makes even a common life bright; that if we have it in us it may be as golden sunlight to some poor one who is in the darkness of ignorance, that is the advantage and the beauty of all good things in our lives, namely, the good it may be unto others. And the beautiful music we may sing or play is not to show what we are or what we can do—it will, of course do these things—but it is to be a blessing to those who listen. And how are blessings bestowed? Out of the heart.

Once there was a nobleman with power and riches. He loved everything. Learning and art and all had he partaken of. But the times were troubled in his country, and for some reason he lost all he had and was imprisoned. Then there was scarcely anything in his life. All he had was the cell, the prison-yard, and, now and again, a word or two with his keeper. The cell was small and gloomy, the keeper silent, the yard confined and so closely paved with cobblestones that one could scarcely see the earth between them.

Yes, indeed, it was a small world and a barren one into which they had forced him. But he had his thoughts, and daily as he walked in his confined yard, they were busy with the past, weaving, weaving. What patterns they made, and he, poor one, was sometimes afraid of them! But still they kept on weaving, weaving.

One day, as he walked in his yard, he noticed that between two of the stones there seemed to be something and he looked at it. With the greatest attention he studied it, then he knelt on the rude stones and looked and looked again. His heart beat and his hands trembled, but yet with a touch as gentle as anyone could give, he moved a grain or two of soil and there, beneath, was something which the poor captive cried out for joy to see—a tiny plant. As if in a new world, and certainly as if another man, he cared daily for the tender little companion that had come to share his loneliness; he thought of it first in the morning and last at night. He gave it of his supply of water and, as a father, he watched over it.

And it grew so that one day he saw that his plant must either die or have more room. And it could not have more room unless a cobblestone were removed. Now this could only be done with the consent of the Emperor. Well, let us not stop to hear about the way he found, but he did get his request to the Emperor and, after a while, what happened do you think? That the plant was given more room? Yes, that is partly it, and the rest is this: the prisoner himself was given more room—he was liberated.

Just because the seed of a beautiful thing came to life in his tiny world he found love for it and a new life, a care, something outside of himself. And it brought him all.

That love which is not given to self reveals the beauty of the world.

In School.

"Every successive generation becomes a living memorial of our public schools, and a living example of their excellence."— Joseph Story.

In these days we learn many things in our schools— even music. They surely must have a purpose, all the studies and the music as well. Let us in this Talk see if we can find what the purpose is.

It costs our Government a great deal to educate the children of the land. There are now nearly twenty million children in our country. That is a number you cannot conceive. But every morning of the year, when it is not a vacation day, you may think of this vast number leaving home and going to school to be taught. I am sure the picture will make us all think how wise a Government is that devotes so much to making us know more, because by learning more we are able to enjoy more, to do more, to be more. And this makes us better citizens.

Year after year, as men study and learn about what is best to have children taught in school, the clearer it becomes that what is given is dictated because of its usefulness. Arithmetic teaches us to calculate our daily affairs. Grammar teaches us to listen and to speak understandingly. Penmanship and Spelling teach us properly to make the signs which represent speech. Geography teaches us of the earth on which we live, and how we may travel about it. History teaches us how to understand the doings of our own day and makes us acquainted with great men of former times, who by striving have earned a place in our remembrance.

As we go on in our school education, taking up new studies, we find to a still greater degree that what we learn is for usefulness. Arithmetic becomes mathematics in general. Grammar is brought before us in other languages, and branches out into the study of Rhetoric and Literature. History is taught us of many lands, particularly of Greece, Rome, and England. And, bit by bit, these various histories merge into one, until, perhaps not until college years or later, the doings of the countries in all the centuries of which we have knowledge is one unbroken story to us. We know the names of lands and of people. Why Greece could love art, why Rome could have conquest; why these countries and all their glories passed away to give place to others; all these things become clear to us. We learn of generals, statesmen, poets, musicians, rulers. Their characters are made clear; their lives are given to us in biography, and year after year the story of the earth and man is more complete, more fascinating, more helpful to us in learning our own day.

Then, besides all these studies, we are taught to do things with the hands. After the Talks we have already had about doing, we know what it means to have training of the hands. It really means the training of the thoughts. We are training the mind to make the hands perform their tasks rightly. It is the same in the science lesson which teaches us to see; actually to use our eyes until we see things. That may not seem to be a difficult task, but there are really very few people who can accurately and properly use their eyes. If there were more, fewer mistakes would be made.

Thus we can see that school work divides its tasks into two general classes:

First, the learning of facts.

Second, the actual doing of things.

You will readily see that to do things properly is possible only when we know facts which tell us how to do them. That shows you at once the wisdom of the education you receive.

Now, let us imagine that school life is over. For many years you have gone faithfully every day to your place, you have done your tasks as honestly as you could, and said your lessons, being wounded no doubt by failures, but gladdened again by successes. Now, when it is all over, what is there of it?

Well, above all things, there is one truth of it which it is wonderful people do not think of more frequently. And that truth is this: The only education we may use in our own life is that which we have ourselves. No longer have we help of companions or teachers. We depend entirely upon our own personal knowledge. If we speak it is our own knowledge of Grammar that is used. We cannot have a book at hand in order to know from it the words we should use. If we make a calculation about money, or do anything with numbers, it must be done from our knowledge of Arithmetic, and it must be right or people will very soon cease to deal with us. Then, if we have a letter from a friend, we must of ourselves know how to read it, and if we have aught to say to another at a distance, we must be able clearly to express ourselves in writing, so that we may make no mistake in our meaning.

And this, likewise, is to be said of all the rest. Our knowledge of History, of Geography, of men of past times, of the boundaries of countries, of cities, of people, of everything, must come from ourselves. And, further yet, according as we have been careful to see in the right way and to do in the right way while we were under instruction in school, so we shall be likely to see and to do when we are not in school, and no longer have someone over us who will kindly and patiently correct our errors, teach us new ways, and give us greater powers. We may, of course, go on learning after our schooldays are ended; and really much of the best education comes then, if we will immediately set about correcting the faults which we find in ourselves.

Indeed, many men have gained the best part of their education after leaving school, where, perhaps, it was their fortune to stay but a short time. But we must remember that the habits of learning, doing, seeking, are gained in early years, and if they are not gained then they rarely come.

Now, what have we learned about schools and school-tasks? We have learned a little of the purpose which lies in the education we receive; that out of it must come the power to do and to know; that is our own power; not that of any one else. We have seen the usefulness of school-studies, and how practical they are in our daily life.

In all this Talk we have said nothing about Music. If, however, we understand what the other studies mean, what their purpose is, we shall learn something which shall be valuable when we come to study the meaning and purpose of music in schools. That shall be our next Talk.

Music in School.

"Become in early years well-informed concerning the extent of the four voices.

"Try, even with a poor voice, to sing at sight without the aid of an instrument; from that your ear will constantly improve. In case, however, that you have a good voice, do not hesitate a moment to cultivate it; and believe, at the same time, that heaven has granted you a valuable gift."

—Robert Schumann.

In the previous Talk we learned two very important facts about school studies. They were these:

I. They are useful.

II. They are useful in proportion to our own (not to anybody else's) real knowledge of them.

We do not study useless subjects, and it is not from our books, nor from our teacher that we go through life, making our way. In other words, the harder we work, the more independent we become; and the more independent we become, the more power we have to help others.

Now, whatever is true about other school studies is likewise true about music. It is given to children in school because it is useful, and because a child can gain power by learning it. Let us see about this.

To one who does not think deeply, it might seem that if any study in school is merely ornamental, that study is music. He might say that all the other studies tend to some practical end in life and business: that one could not add, nor read, nor transact business, nor write a letter any more correctly by knowing music. It is only an unthinking person—none other—who would say that.

Of the usefulness of all the school studies we have spoken. We need only to take a few steps along the pleasant road, about which we have had so many Talks, and we shall see how much music means in life. To us it is already plain. Music is a new world, to enter which cultivates new senses, teaches us to love the beautiful, and makes us watchful of two of the most important things in life: the thoughts and the heart. We must have exact thoughts or the music is not made a right, and the heart may be what it will, music tells all about it. Therefore, let it be good.

But music in school brings us to daily tasks in tone. What do we learn? After the difficulties of reading the notes and making the voice responsive are somewhat overcome, we study for greater power in both, the one-, two-, or three-part exercises and songs; the exercises for skill and the songs to apply the skill, and make us acquainted with the music of great masters.

In one Talk, one of the first, we spoke of the major scale. It has eight tones only, and though it has existed for many hundreds of years, no one has yet dreamed of all the wonderful tone-pictures which are contained in it. It is out of it that all the great composers have written their works, and for centuries to come men will find in it beauties great, and pure, and lasting.

As we sing in school, we are learning to put the major scale to some use. It calls upon us in the melodies which it expresses, to be careful that each tone shall be right in length, in pitch, in loudness, in place. We must sing exactly with the others, not offensively loud, nor so softly as to be of no service. And this demands precision of us; and precision demands thought. And if we are singing to gain a better use of voice we must, in every sound we make, have our thoughts exactly upon what we are doing. This is Concentration. If, on the other hand, we are trying our skill on a song, we shall have, in addition, to be careful to give the right expression, to sing not only the tones clearly, but the words, to feel the true sentiment both of the poem and of the music, and to express from our hearts as much of the meaning of poet and composer as we understand. All these things are more particularly required of us if we are singing in parts. The melody must be properly sustained and must not cover the under parts; while the under parts themselves should never intrude upon the melody, nor fail to be a good background for it. The singing of part music is one of the best ways to train the attention—that is, to get Concentration. As we sing our part we must have in mind these things:

I. To keep to it and not be drawn away by another part.

II. To give the part we sing its due prominence.

III. Never to destroy the perfect equality of the parts by unduly hastening or holding back.

IV. To remember that each part is important. The other singers have as much to think of and to do as we have, and they are entitled to just as much praise.

V. To be alert to take up our part at exactly the right place.

VI. To put the full meaning of the poet and of the composer into every word and tone.

These, after all, are only a few of the things; but from them we may learn this, that to sing (and to play is quite the same) is one of the most delicate tasks we can learn to perform, requiring attention from us in many ways at the same time. Even now the usefulness of music is clear, for the faculties we learn to employ in music form a power that can be applied in anything.

But music has even a greater reward for us than this. It presents to us many kinds of thoughts and pictures,—of bravery, of thoughtfulness, of gaiety, and others without number—and then it demands that we shall study so as to sing them truthfully from our hearts. And when we can do this music is then a joy to us and to others.

Now we see that music, just like the other studies, is useful and gives us the power to do something. And besides its use and power it is, perhaps more than any other study, the greatest means of giving happiness to others. But of that there is yet a word to be said. That shall be our next Talk.

How One Thing Helps Another.

"Music washes away from the soul the dust of everyday life."—Berthold Auerbach.

Just at the end of our Talk about Music in School, I said that music was the most powerful of all the studies for giving joy to others. In this Talk we shall try to learn what the studies do for each other.

Once more—and we must never get tired if the same thought comes again and again—let us remember that music is thought expressed in tone. Classic music is great and strong thought; poor, unworthy music is weak, perhaps wrong or mean thought.

Further, we have learned that thought may be good and pure, and yet that of itself is not sufficient. It must be well expressed. In short, to thought of the right sort we must add knowledge, so that it may be set before others in the right way.

Now, it is true that the more knowledge we have, the more we can do with music. We can put more meaning into it; we can better perform all the exacting duties it demands; we can draw more meaning from its art, and we can see more clearly how great a genius the composer is. Besides these things, a well-trained mind gets more thoughts from a subject than an untrained mind. Some day you will see this more clearly by observing how much better you will be able to understand your own language by possessing a knowledge of Greek and Latin.

All the school studies have a use, to be sure—a direct use—in giving us something to help us in life in one way and another. But besides this, we get another help from study; namely, the employment of the mind in the right way. For the right way of doing things which are worthy of the heart, gives power and good. It is the wrong way of doing things that causes us trouble. Some studies demand exactness above all this,—like the study of Arithmetic—others a good memory,—like History—others tax many faculties, as we have seen in our Talk about School Music.

Some of the studies are particularly valuable to us at once because they make us do. They may be called doing studies. In Arithmetic there is a result, and only one result, to be sought. In Grammar every rule we learn is to be applied in our speech. Manual training demands judgment and the careful use of the hands. Penmanship is a test for the hand, but History is a study touching the memory more than the doing faculty.

School music, you see at once, is a doing study. Not only that, it is full of life, attractive, appealing to the thoughts in many ways, and yet it is a hearty study—by that I mean a study for the heart.

If you have noticed in your piano music the Italian words which are given at the beginning of compositions, you may have thought how expressive most of them are of the heart and of action. They are doing words particularly. Allegro is cheerful; that is its true meaning. It directs us to make the music sound cheerful as we sing it or play it. What for? So that the cheerfulness of the composer shall be for us and for other people. And Vivace is not merely quickly, but vivaciously. Now what does vivacious mean? It means what its root-word *vivere* means, to live. It is a direction that the music must be full of life; and the true life of happiness and freedom from care is meant. So with Moderato, a doing word which tells us very particularly how to do; namely, not too fast, spoiling it by haste, nor too slowly, so that it seems to drag, but in a particular way, that is, with moderation.

Music takes its place as a doing study; and as we have already discovered, its doing is of many kinds, all requiring care. Singing or playing is doing; reading the notes is doing; studying out the composer's meaning is doing; making others feel it is doing; everything is doing; and doing is true living, provided it is unselfish.

Let us see if there is not a simple lesson in all this. To seek it we shall have to say old thoughts over again. Music itself uses the same tones over and over again; it is by doing so that we begin to understand tone a little.

The school studies try the mind; with the tasks increased bit by bit, the mind is made stronger. Thus is Strength gained. By the tasks demanding exactness, the thoughts must not be scattered everywhere, but centered upon the thing to be done. Thus is Concentration gained.

By making the hand work with care and a definite purpose, Skill is gained. By demanding of the thoughts that they must seek out all the qualities of an object, Attention is gained. By placing things and signs for things before us, we are taught to See. By educating us in sounds, we are taught to Listen. When we have a task that admits of a single correct result, we are taught Exactness.

Now, from all we have learned in these Talks about music it must be clear that all these qualities are just what are needed in music:

I. Strength of thought for Real doing.

II. Concentration for Right doing.

III. Skill for Well doing.

IV. Seeing and listening for the cultivation of Attention.

V. Correctness for the Manner of doing.

We sought for a simple lesson. It is this:

Let us learn all we can that is right and worthy for the strengthening of the mind, for the cultivation of the heart, for the good and joy of others; for these things are the spirit of music.

The Child at Play.

"When the long day is past, the steps turn homeward."

Once a child played on the sea-shore. The waves sang and the sand shone and the pebbles glistened. There was light everywhere; light from the blue sky, and from the moving water, and from the gleaming pebbles.

The little one, in its happiness, sang with the murmuring sea and played with the stones and the shells that lay about. Joy was everywhere and the child was filled with it.

But the day passed. And the little one grieved in its heart to leave the beautiful place. Delight was there and many rare things that one could play with and enjoy.

The child could not leave them all. Its heart ached to think of them lying there alone by the sea. And it thought:

"I will take the pebbles and the shells with me and I will try to remember the sunlight and the song of the sea."

So it began to fill its little hands. But it saw that after as many as possible were gathered together there were yet myriads left. And it had to leave them.

Tired and with a sore heart it trudged homeward, its hands filled to overflowing with the pebbles that shone in the sun on the sea-shore. Now, however, they seemed dull. And because of this, the child did not seem to regret it so much if now and then one fell. "There are still some left in my hands," it thought.

At length it came near to its home; so very tired, the little limbs could scarcely move. And one who loved the child came out smiling to welcome it. The little one went up close and rested its tired head; and opening its little hand, soiled with the sea and the sand, said:

"Look, mother, I still have one. May I go for the others some day?"

And the mother said:

"Yes, thou shalt go again."

And the child fell asleep to dream of the singing sea and of the sunlight, for these were in its heart.

YOUNG PEOPLE'S

HISTORY OF MUSIC

WITH

BIOGRAPHIES OF FAMOUS MUSICIANS

BY

JAMES C. MACY

BOSTON:

Copyright, 1886, by

OLIVER DITSON & CO.

NEW YORK: PHILA: CHICAGO:

C. H. DITSON & CO.   J. E. DITSON & CO.   LYON & HEALY.

YOUNG PEOPLE'S

HISTORY OF MUSIC.

CHAPTER I.

THE MUSICAL ART IN ITS EARLIEST FORM —
ANCIENT CHURCH MUSIC — FIRST SYSTEMS
OF NOTATION.

ALTHOUGH the most ancient of the earth's
inhabitants indulged in song and played upon
rude musical instruments, yet it was not until
the beginning of the Christian era that music
began to grow and develop, and be called an
art. It became a part of the ceremonies of the
first churches, and, as it thus grew in importance,
men saw the necessity of making a regular system of signs, so that all could sing together the
same hymn. Music became a written language,
we might say. To the church we owe its development, and with the church we must follow its
course.

Owing to the low character of the Roman
(heathen) festivities, where musical *instruments*

had been used, such instruments were not
allowed in the ceremonies of the first Christian
congregations. The music consisted of singing
only. As the churches increased in number and
power, however, instrumental music grew into
favor.

The singing in these first churches consisted
of the *antiphonal*, or *alternate* chant, sung by two
divisions, or choirs of people ; that is, one division sang a verse of the psalm, the other division
sang the next verse, and so on, alternately.
Sometimes a single voice sang a verse, and the
people responded.

Some of the oldest church music is called
plain song, or *Gregorian chant*, and is supposed
to have been introduced by St. Gregory the
Great (A D. 590), although this is disputed by
some writers.

The most ancient method of writing music, or
representing different tones by certain signs
(called notation), was probably invented by
Alypius for the music of ancient Greece. He
used the letters of the Greek alphabet, placed in
various positions. Afterwards, another Greek
scholar, Aristides, improved this system. The
Greek Church also had its way of indicating
musical sounds, but it was a very confusing

method and led to much difficulty. At a later
date these systems gave place to others, as we
shall see.

In mediæval times the general custom was to
write signs over the words that were to be sung
or chanted; here is a specimen of such writing:

PROBABLE SOLUTION

Cœl - li cœl - lo - rum   lau - da - te   De - um.

These signs written over the words are called
neumes, (noo-mes), from the Greek word *numa*
or *pneuma*, meaning a breath, and were in use
until the latter part of the 12th century, taking
on various shapes and gradually approaching the
finally adopted system of notation.

Hucbaldus, a monk of St. Amand in Flanders,
at the end of the 9th and at the beginning of
the 10th centuries, invented the next system of
notation. This consisted of a ladder of letters
like the following :—

A		a			
G	da	te		num	
F	Lau		mi		de
E		do			
D				e	coelis

These Latin words are: *Laudate Dominum*

de cœlis — "Praise the Lord of Heaven." You observe that the syllables are placed in different positions on the "ladder" in order to give each its proper tone. This division of syllables was the chief objection to the system; and another difficulty was the doubling and trebling of the vowels when there happened to be two or three tones to one syllable. However, the scale consisted of only four or five tones, and so the singers, or chanters, managed to perform the service very creditably, no doubt.

The next musical system in order of date was the hexachord, a series of six tones, indicated by letters and syllables on lines and spaces. The scale, of course, was quite limited. It is said that Guido Aretino, or d'Arezzo, a monk in the Bendictine monastery at Pomposa, Italy, in the 11th century, invented this system; but some writers dispute this claim and give the credit to early English scholars.

The syllables used in the hexachord system were, *Ut, Re, Mi, Fa, Sol, La, and Sa;* and these were taken from the lines of a hymn to St. John the Baptist, thus : —

Ut queant laxis	*Solve* polluti
*Re*sonare fibris,	*La*bia reati,
*Mi*ra gestorum	*Sancta* Johannes.
*Fa*muli tuorum :	

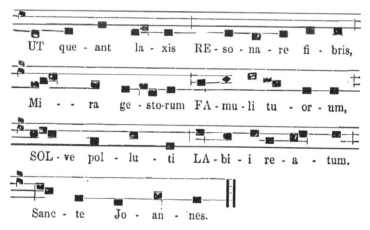

UT que - ant la - xis RE - so - na - re fi - bris,

Mi - - ra ge - sto-rum FA - mu - li tu - or - um,

SOL - ve pol - lu - ti LA - bi - i re - a - tum.

Sanc - te Jo - an - nes.

Guido d'Arezzo also adopted, about this time, a system of writing signs upon colored lines, so that the eye could distinguish the position of a sign or tone very readily. But this method was not long in use.

It soon became plain that some method of time division or measurement should be adopted. Before this period there had been no time-measurement, no rhythm, in music; only an accent upon certain words and syllables of the chant; for the neumes were merely signs of intonation. Finally, in the beginning of the 13th century, Franco de Colona* proposed and

---

* Franco of Cologne; called by some, Franco of Paris. The place of his birth has not been ascertained. He is supposed to have been a scholar of the cathedral of Liege.

arranged a plan of notation and time-division in music, which was probably the foundation of all that was afterwards accomplished. The staff consisted of four lines, and the notes were like these :—

The *long*, the *breve*, the *semi-breve*.

In course of time the number of musical figures was increased to six, as follows :—

1, the *double long ;* 2, the *long ;* 3, the *breve ;* 4, the *semi-breve ;* 5, the *minim ;* 6, the *semi-minim.*

Towards the middle of the sixteenth century, notes were formed *round*, and continue in this shape at the present day.

Mensural music (music divided into measures and time-beats) began to receive attention during Franco's time, for his writings and inventions had their effect. Indeed, Dr. Ritter says, in his "History of Music," that "the importance of Franco's teachings cannot be too highly estimated ; we are even justified in dating from his time the real beginning of *contrapuntal* art." *

* Contrapuntal art is the art of writing " point against point " — or *counterpoint* — several voices or parts moving together in harmonious order. Notes were often called *points* by old writers.

Mensural music, as explained by Franco, was generally introduced by church singers and theorists, and a difference was observed between mensural music and the old *Gregorian chant*, or *plain song* The music of hymns and chants began to be written in parts for two or more voices, and musical sounds were more agreeably blended or harmonized.

It took several centuries of patient labor and experiment to bring all this about. Those old monks, who studied and worked with such devotion and industry, did not dream that they were sowing seed which should grow into such beautiful art-forms and become the source of so much delicious enjoyment.

CHAPTER II.

Folk-Song—Troubadours and Minnesingers.

All nations, from the earliest times, have had their own peculiar songs—*folk-songs*, or people's songs, we call them — beginning, nobody knows where or how, but seemingly coming from the very depths of the human heart. These songs express the emotions of the people, as produced by occurrences in every-day life, or by certain national events. .

"There is no doubt that the ancient nations — the Hebrews, the Greeks, the Romans, etc.— possessed many folk-songs ; yet none of them, as far as we can judge, have come down to us ; and, although it is presumed that some of these songs found their way into the Christian church, history fails to give any distinct proof of it." *

The folk-song † and the Gregorian song, or chant (mentioned in the preceding chapter), constitute the foundation of our musical art. Early composers made some of the folk-songs the themes (or subjects) of very elaborate and

* Ritter.   † In German, *volkslied.*

important compositions, and in many ways can we trace the development of art-form back to the old folk-song.

The melodies of the folk-songs of the middle ages have not all been preserved, though we find the words of some of them in old chronicles, especially of the German and French.

In the twelfth century, one class of folk-song was composed and sung by the *troubadours* * of France, Italy, and Spain, and by the *minnesingers* † of Germany. The troubadours were young men of high degree, often knights, who composed and sang their own songs, (nearly always love-songs addressed to some fair lady). "Gayety, or joy, was a state of mind regarded by the troubadours as corresponding with that of religious grace. The end of their profession was the service of religion, honor, and woman, in deed and in song. One of their mottoes was, 'Love and religion protect all the virtues'; another ran, 'My soul to God, my life for the king, my heart for my lady, my honor for myself.'

"The troubadour most esteemed was he who could invent, compose, and accompany his own songs; but those who were unable to play the

* From the Provençal (French) *trobar*, to invent or find.
† Love-singers, (German).

instruments of the period—the harp, lute, viola, or citara (the ancient Irish rota or crowth)—were accompanied by a salaried minstrel; in the South, these minstrels were termed jongleurs, or violars. If a troubadour was not gifted with a fine voice, he employed a singer to perform the songs which he could create, but not sing."[*]

From place to place, from court to court, the troubadour traveled and sang, and was held in high estimation, even by crowned rulers; indeed, some of the nobles and kings themselves practised the troubadour's art of writing verses and composing melodies.

The *minnesingers*, who flourished in Germany, composed and sang their songs in the Swabian dialect (then the court language), playing their own accompaniments on a viol. The minnesingers employed a charming variety of tunes in different metres, while the troubadours nearly always sang in the same rhythm and adapted their melodies to it.

The art of these troubadours, minstrels, and minnesingers, called the *gay science*, was brought to Europe from the East, probably by way of Spain, and its duration was about two hundred years (from 1090–1290), the period when East-

---

[*] Fanny Raymond Ritter, "Essay on the Troubadours."

ern customs began to influence and give tone to
those of western Europe, and while chivalry
began to redeem men from barbarism. Warton
in his "History of English Poetry," says of the
troubadours : "They introduced a love of reading, and created a popular taste for poetry.
Their verses became the chief amusement of
princes and feudal lords, whose courts had now
begun to assume a great brilliancy."

In Germany, some time after the passing
away of minnesinging, there arose a class of
singers known as the *meister-singers* (master-
singers), an association or *guild* of villagers,
tradespeople, etc. No one could be admitted
to this society unless he had invented a new
style of rhyme. The headquarters, or chief
place, of this guild was at Nuremberg. Hans
Sachs, a shoemaker of that town, was one of
the most celebrated meister-singers, and there
have been a number of poems, stories, and an
opera written, with Hans Sachs for the subject.
These meister-singers, however, did nothing to
benefit the musical art, and were in no wise as
interesting as their predecessors, the troubadours and minnesingers.

CHAPTER III.

THE FLEMISH SCHOOL — SCHOOL OF THE NETHERLANDERS.

For more than a century after Franco's teaching, music remained in nearly the same condition; the crusades, which occurred at about that time, occupied the attention of European nations, and we find no important musical discovery or theory of that period, although we know of several writers who attracted attention, but who failed to improve on the systems already established.

We pass on to the close of the fourteenth and beginning of the fifteenth centuries, when new forms and values of time in music were fast growing into *contrapuntal* art,* and when (in 1502) the invention of printing music-notes † with metal types helped to spread a knowledge of the art, and aided composers in bringing their works to the notice of the people.

---

* See definitions, page 12 in foot-note.

† The inventor of music-types was Ottavio Petrucci, of Fossombrone, Italy.

We shall describe the manner of printing music, in a chapter further on.

In France, Italy, Germany and England, were writers and composers who did much at this time toward perfecting the art of counterpoint; but the French and Flemish (Dutch) schools — methods, style — were the most celebrated, having several distinguished composers who wrote at different periods between the years 1420 and 1520, or thereabouts. The most celebrated of these were William Dufay, Joannes Okeghem (or Ockenheim), Josquin des Pres, and Adrian Willært. Their works were chiefly masses, motets, etc., for the use of the Catholic church, and the oldest specimens of this style of musical composition are in the pope's chapel at Rome, and were written by Dufay, who was a tenor singer in the Sistine chapel from 1380 to 1432. His compositions are remarkable specimens of counterpoint as it appeared in those early days.

A very celebrated composer and teacher of the Flemish school, after Dufay, was Okeghem. We have no reliable date concerning his birth, but it was probably as early as 1415. He was at one time a singer in the Antwerp cathedral, and, after giving up his position there, entered the service of the king of France. He is said to have served three kings of France, in forty years, and lived to be nearly one hundred years old.

Okeghem was one of the greatest masters of *canon* * and counterpoint. He was, perhaps, the most celebrated teacher of his time, as pupils were so anxious to learn of him that they came from all parts to enjoy his instruction.

The next great composer of the Flemish school, or school of the Netherlanders, as it is called, was Josquin des Pres.† He was the greatest genius of all the early writers, in fact, and his compositions were used in preference to those of all other musicians at that period. Martin Luther very much admired Josquin's music. It is related that Luther once said, after hearing one of Josquin's compositions performed, " He makes the notes do as *he* pleases; most other composers have to obey the notes."

Josquin was a singer in the pope's chapel at Rome from 1471 to 1484. He was at the court of Louis XII of France, in 1497; but afterwards,

---

* A composition for two or more parts or voices, the parts commencing one after another, and imitating each other. The word is derived from the Greek, and means simply law or rule.

† Born in the year 1445; died at Condé, 1521.

it is said, he entered the service of the Emperor Maximilian.

Adrian Willært* was another composer and teacher of music, whose influence later in the period of which we are writing, was great and beneficial. He was director of music in the church of St. Mark, at Venice, in the year 1527.

Two great masters, Palestrina and Orlando di Lasso, who received their knowledge through the Flemish and French schools, I shall notice further on, in the chapter devoted to Italy.

The composers of the Flemish school, who taught and wrote during the period when the Netherlanders were taking the lead in musical learning, and were teaching other nations, brought to a high standard the forms in music known as *counterpoint, canon,* and *fugue.*† A broad basis was laid, on which all musical progress rests, and on which the greatest musical compositions have been built. The use of movable metal types made music-printing cheaper than the old way of printing from wood.

---

* Born in the year 1490 ; died in 1562.

† Pronounced f-*yoog ;* from the Latin word *fuga,* flight. One voice or part in a fugue is followed closely by another, taking "flight." In the early days of music, *canon* and *fugue* were the same, but musicians now treat them as separate forms.

The invention soon became generally known and used, especially in Germany ; and, as a result of all this, the different masses,* motets,† and chansons ‡ of the masters were speedily placed before a music-loving people.

And now, before proceeding further with our history proper, let us, in the next chapter, see how music was and is printed.

* The music which accompanies the ceremony of the Catholic church.

† Short, musical composition with Scriptural words. (*Italian.*)

‡ Songs (*French.*)

CHAPTER IV.

MUSIC PRINTING.

In 1503, Ottaviano Petrucci, (born at Fossombrone, Italy, in the year 1466), established a printing press at Venice, where he published some masses. He afterwards removed to Fossombrone, where he obtained a patent from Leo X for the invention of movable metal types for printing music. Before this, music had been printed from engraved wooden blocks, and the characters appeared very rough and indistinct. Here is a specimen of printing before Petrucci's invention, taken from a book printed by Wynkin de Worde, at Westminster, England, in 1495: —

In another old book, printed with movable types, the notes were slightly improved, and the printer thought it necessary to prefix an explanation of the types he employed, which he does in the following words: "In this booke is conteyned so much of the order of Common Praier as is to be song in Churches, wherein are used only these iiij. sortes of notes : —

The first note is a strene note and is a breue, the second note is a square note and is a semybreue, the iij. a prycke and is a mynymne. And when there is a prycke by the square note, that prycke is half as muche as the note that goeth before it. The iiij. is a close, and is vsed at only yᵉ end of a verse."

The invention of Petrucci aided printers in making clearer and handsomer looking impres-sions, and the movable types soon grew into favor everywhere.

At first, all music-notes were printed sepa-rately ; that is to say, all the notes in a measure, no matter how many, or of what value, were distinct, like these : ♩ ♪♪. About the year 1660, John Pleyford (English) invented what he called the new "tied note," on this principle: ♫ ♫ ♬ which made music appear neater to the eye, and easier to read. Other improve-ments were made, from time to time, and the process of printing music from types became general in all the enlightened European nations.

Young People's History of Music.

At the commencement of this present century, new and more graceful shapes were given to the notes printed from types; the art progressed, and to-day the business of music-printing is an important one.

There are two processes of printing music now in general use, the engraved plate process and the type process. The plates on which music-notes were at first engraved (in the seventeenth century), were made of copper, and were expensive. The plates used to-day are of a composition of metal, containing tin. Engraved notes are, by some, considered more elegant than those produced by types; the curved lines and marks of expression used in music are often plainer, and more correctly placed, in engraved plates; but the "words" of a song or other vocal piece never look well in this process.

The notes and other characters in engraved plates of the present time are made with "punches" of the shape required. This is not strictly engraving, and is not to be compared with the old, laborious way. The process of printing from these plates is a slow one, and when many copies of a piece are to be rapidly printed, the type process is used. An engraved plate cannot be used on a steam press; there is

142

a special kind of press, worked by hand, on which the plates are placed.

The process of printing from type is as follows : Music types are " set up " or placed together to form the desired pages of music, and *stereotype* or *electrotype* plates are made from them. *Stereotyping* is done by taking a mould or impression in either plaster or clay, from the type that is " set up " to form the page. Melted metal is poured into this mould, making an exact copy of the type-page, all in one solid plate.

Electrotyping consists in taking a mould in wax instead of plaster or clay. A delicate film of black lead (plumbago) is formed on the mould, in order to conduct electricity ; the mould is then put into a solution of sulphate of copper, and a current of electricity from a dynamic-electro machine is kept constantly passing through the solution for two or three hours, which causes a deposit of copper on the mould. When sufficiently thick, the " shell " of copper is removed from the mould, and placed face downward on a level surface, and molten metal poured on, to give the plate thickness and strength. The plate is then shaved to an even thickness and made ready for the press. Electrotyping costs a trifle more than stereotyping, but will wear more than twice as long.

Music is not printed direct from the type, on account of the high cost of music type, and for the reason that, when plates are made, any number of editions can be printed without any further expense or delay except for press work. Electrotype or stereotype music plates are put on ordinary printing presses, and printed by steam the same as plain book work. The music and words which are to appear in the printed page, appear in the plate as a raised surface; rollers which are covered very evenly with ink are rolled across the plate, leaving ink on the raised characters; a sheet of paper is then pressed on, and the ink adhering to the sheet produces the printed page. After the plates are made ready, the whole operation, except feeding the sheets to the press, is done by steam power, and at a considerable speed; and as presses and paper are both made large, a great many pages are printed on one sheet, making the cost of printing very low.

A page of music type consists of a great many small pieces, joined together to represent continuous lines and characters. For instance, this group of notes ♩♩♩ is composed of twenty-four pieces, thus : ♩♩♩ When a font of type is

new, the joints are not noticeable ; but the sharp
corners of the type very quickly become worn,
and this worn type must be replaced by new, or
the quality of the work deteriorates. The skill
and judgment shown in allotting the proper
space between the notes, the breaking of joints,
the length of stems, and general care bestowed,
all contribute to the desired end. Below is
given an exact fac-simile of a few measures
taken from a book recently issued : —

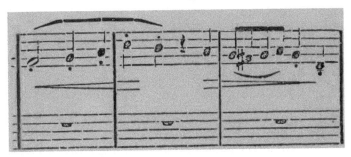

Here is the same, set in a different style of the
art : —

The preceding illustrations show the difference between the high and low grades of music typography at the present time. *

---

* The foregoing facts relating to the stereotype and electrotype processes, are taken by permission from " Music Typography," by F. H. Gilson of Boston.

CHAPTER V.

THE MADRIGAL.

From the school of the Netherlanders let us pass to the music of other European nations, as it appeared at the period when Adrian Willært (mentioned in a previous chapter) was the most influential teacher and composer that the Flemish school had produced.

These Dutch masters had taken the lead in music for more than a century, and the musicians of the Netherlands were found in control of the chapels and church choirs throughout Europe. But the cultivation of the art had not been neglected in England, France, Spain, Germany, and Italy, during all this time. In England, vocal and instrumental music had been studied with care; counterpoint was well understood; and, as early as 1420, there were able composers in that country, the most famous being John Dunstable. Many fine motets, anthems and chants were composed by English musicians, such as Thomas Tallis, William Bird, Thomas Morley, and others.

Young People's History of Music.

The beginning of the sixteenth century, therefore, saw the art of music very well advanced in Europe ; the writers of the times took special delight in the study of part-writing, or in arranging melodies to be sung by several voices, all harmonizing and blending in the most pleasing way. In short, as an English writer has said, "We find, at this period, science and popular melody working together for a common purpose." The result of this was the *madrigal*, a much admired form of polyphonic * composition, which originated in the Flemish school (Adrian Willært probably being the composer who first gave it artistic attention), and which found great favor also in Italy. The Flemish and Italian madrigals, finding their way into England, flourished there with greater success than in any other country.

The *madrigal* † is the folk-song in a very artistic dress, combining counterpoint, fugue, etc.,

Polyphonic, a term given to all compositions consisting of a number of parts.

† There is a difference of opinion as to the origin of this word. Webster's definition is as follows : " *Madrigal*, a word derived from *mandra*, a flock, a herd of cattle." Hence the madrigal would seem to be a pastoral, or " country " folk-song.

148

and is generally written for five and six voices. The words usually express hopes, griefs, desires, love, according to the poet's fancy, and are set to very simple yet expressive melodies, "treated" (as musicians say) in the contrapuntal manner, which we have explained. Some of the old English and Italian madrigals are very beautiful and expressive; some of them quaint and curious; all of them very interesting to the lover of music.

In a book of madrigals published by Archadelt, at Venice, in the year 1538, there are some very lovely specimens of this style of composition. The volume is in the British museum, among other rare and interesting books. One of the old madrigals in that collection is by Archadelt himself, and we here give a portion of it.

IL BIANCO E DOLCE CIGNO.

(THE WHITE AND LOVELY SWAN.)

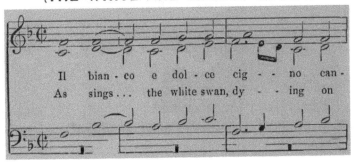

Il bian - co e dol - ce cig - - no can -
As sings ... the white swan, dy - - ing on

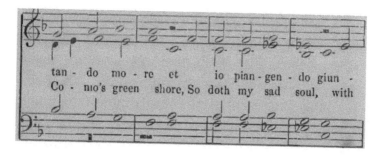

tan - do mo - re et io pian - gen - do giun -
Co - mio's green shore, So doth my sad soul, with

ge al fin del vi - ver mi - - o, et io piangen-
sigh-ing and cry - ing, once more her plaintive song

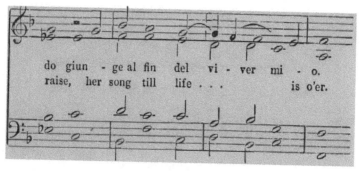

do giun - ge al fin del vi - ver mi - o.
raise, her song till life . . . is o'er.

In England the madrigal became firmly established; it formed a national "school" or style
of music, and the English madrigals are not surpassed by those of any other country. Thomas

Morley, Michael Este, Weelkes, John Benet, Hilton, Wilbye, Orlando Gibbons, Pierson, George Kirbye, William Bird, and Richard Edwardes, wrote some fine madrigals, which are much prized by English people and by musicians generally. Here are several good examples from the compositions of those old authors: —

THE SILVER SWAN.

By ORLANDO GIBBONS, A.D., 1593.

Leaning her breast against the reed-y shore,

Thus sang her first and last, and sang no more.

NOW IS THE MONTH OF MAYING.

THOMAS MORLEY, 1595.

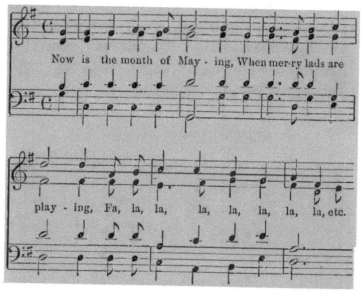

THE FALLING OUT OF FAITHFUL FRIENDS.

By RICHARD EDWARDS, 1560.

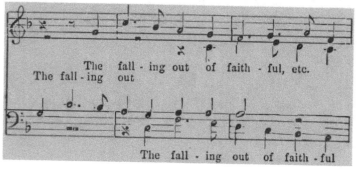

HOW MERRILY WE LIVE.

By MICHAEL ESTE, 1600.

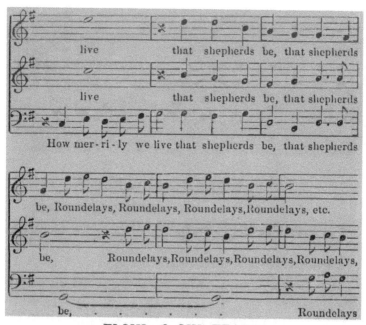

FLOW, O MY TEARS.

By JOHN BENET, A.D., 1598.

We find the madrigal mentioned in Shakespeare's plays; indeed, it was during his time and in the reign of "good Queen Elizabeth" that it began to flourish in England. The glees, catches, rounds, and several other styles of vocal music, which seem to be peculiarly English, have grown from the madrigal, and have become well known in our own country, the English glees and "part-songs" being favorites with many singing-societies. A good description of the madrigal, and the necessary "varietie" in its construction, is thus given in the quaint old way by Thomas Morley, who, writing in the year 1597, tells us that, —

" As for the Musicke, it is next unto the Motet, the most artificiall and to men of Vnderstanding the most delightfull. If therefore you will compose in this Kind you must possesse your selfe with an amorus humor (for in no coposition shall you proue admirable except you put on, and possesse your selfe wholy with that vaine wherein you compose) so that you must in your Musicke be wauering * like the wind, sometime wanton, sometime drooping, sometime graue † and staide, otherwhile effeminat, you may maintaine points and reuert ‡ them, vse triplaes,§ and shew the uttermost of your varietie, and the more varietie you show the better shall you please."

* Wavering.　† Grave.　‡ Reverse.　§ Triplets.

CHAPTER VI.

Italy — Palestrina — Orlando Di Lasso — Italian Masters.

Italy has always been called the "source of art." We have seen that Gregory, Guido and Hucbaldus were the first to advance the musical art an important step, while Petrucci, in a later time, brought forward the means of printing music from movable types; but for two centuries or more, from the thirteenth to the sixteenth, at least, the Flemish and French made the most important advances, and their composers and singers were found in all the Italian churches.

Toward the middle of the sixteenth century the Italian schools again came prominently forward. The oldest is that of Rome; the next that of Venice; while Naples and Lombardy follow. These different "schools," founded, of course, upon the Flemish, became much celebrated in all branches of the musical art.

Probably the first Italian composer who became a real master of counterpoint was Constanzo

Festa, who was a singer in the Sistine Chapel at Rome in 1517, and who during his life was very much esteemed and beloved, as man and musician.

Giovanni Pierluigi da Palestrina was at the head of the school in Rome. The date of his birth has been placed in the year 1524, but there seems to be no certainty with regard to this. We may conclude that, as his name implies, the *place* of his birth was Palestrina — *da* (of) Palestrina. He was a pupil of Claude Goudimel, a French master.

. About the year 1555 he was admitted as a singer into the Pope's Chapel at Rome ; at the age of thirty-three he was elected chapel-master of the church of Santa Maria Maggiore, in the same city ; in 1571 he was appointed chapel-master at St. Peter's ; and he died in the year 1594.

Palestrina's music was composed chiefly for the Church of Rome — masses, motets, etc. ; and the number of his compositions is very great ; in the list there are ninety-three *masses* alone !

" In Palestrina's works Catholic church music found its greatest and purest revelation," says Dr. Ritter ; " they mark the culminating point, and at the same time the close, of a great and unique epoch in our musical art."

And now we come to one who was the greatest of all the masters of the sixteenth century, and who seemed to combine in his great gifts all the best musical elements of each European nation, so that he could not be called specially Italian, German, or French composer. Orlando di Lasso, or Orlandus Lassus, was born at Mons, in Hainault, in the year 1520. At the age of seven he began his education, and a year or two later exhibited a fondness for music, which he soon understood. He joined the choir-boys in the Cathedral of St. Nicolas, in his native town, and was three times stolen or kidnapped on account of his fine voice. Some of the historians tell us that it was a common thing for young singers to be forced away from their parents and kept in the service of princes. Twice his good parents sought and found him; but the third time he desired to remain with Ferdinand de Gonsaga, who took him to Italy. Here he received a fine musical education, and finally went to Rome, where he taught successfully, and where he was chapel-master at the Church of St. John Lateran, when only twenty-one years of age. Albert V, of Bavaria, called him to Munich in 1557, where he was chapel-master at the court until the time of his death, which took place in 1594.

Orlando di Lasso was the greatest musician of his time ; none of the masters who lived during the same period had such a great will, such a clear mind, or such a mastery of all that belonged to his art. He was seldom unsuccessful in his compositions, and equally great both in the lyric * and epic † styles. He composed more than seven hundred different works, which included masses and motets for the church, and songs, madrigals, etc., in Latin, Italian, German and French. A statue in honor of this famous old composer has been erected at Mons, his birthplace.

Cyprian de Rore was another eminent musician of this period, and was like Orlando di Lasso in some respects, though not his equal in genius.

Until the beginning of the present century, the schools of Italy were superior to any other in Europe ; in singing, especially, the Italians excelled, and the number of excellent singers that they have produced can scarcely be reckoned.

Beside the old masters already mentioned, who taught and wrote in Italy, there is a long list of

* Drama and music combined. Opera.
† Illustrative of events.

eminent composers, teachers and performers (some of them great masters), of whom Italy may justly be proud. *Gabrieli*, Monteverde, Allegri, Freseobaldi, Lulli, *Stradella*, *Scarlatti*, Marcello, Astorga, Durante, *Pergolese*, Jomelli, *Piccini*, Salieri, *Clementi*, *Cimarosa*, *Cherubini*, Spontini, Paganini (the great master of the violin), Rossini (see page 99) Donizetti, Bellini and Verdi (see page 129) the great composers of operas, — all these are famous in musical history.

CHAPTER VII.

FRANCE AND SPAIN.

France, at the revival of the arts, towards the close of the fourteenth century, followed the example of the Flemish, and was ably represented by Du Fay, Regis, Caron, Binchois and other French musicians. The eminence of the French school lasted during the reign of Francis I; but the religious troubles, which began about the year 1550, and during which there were bloody wars and destruction or profanation of churches, as well as the death of many master-musicians, very nearly crushed the musical art in France, so that, at the end of the reign of Henry IV there was a very gloomy prospect. Louis XIII was fond of music; but Cardinal Richelieu, who was really the ruler, did not patronize it. In fact, for more than a century music was generally neglected in France.

At length the reign of Louis XIV commenced, when that prince, who was passionately fond of music, and sang and played well on the guitar, patronized the art which he himself loved so much. Lulli, a Florentine, introduced music into France as it then existed in Italy; and it seemed to receive a new existence. It was re-established in the churches, the theatres and concerts; and since that time it has been constantly cultivated with more or less success.

The greatest glory of the French musicians is in dramatic music. They were not precisely the inventors of it, but, by borrowing the dramatic melody of the Italians, and combining it with that of their own nation, they formed a melody peculiar to themselves, and of an excellent character; and, by applying this to well-imagined and well-written poems, they have produced a style of lyric drama that has been much celebrated.

Lulli, Boieldieu, Auber, Méhul, Hérold Halévy and Berlioz were celebrated French composers of opera; and those now living, who are famous for their operatic works, are Charles Gounod and Ambroise Thomas. The most noted French musical theorist and scholar was Jean Philippe Rameau.

Spain has never been famous for its musicians; indeed, musical culture of the higher order seems to have been entirely neglected since the sixteenth century. In those early times there were some excellent Spanish singers and composers in the Pope's Chapel at Rome. The Spanish people are possessed of a poetic nature, and have shown great talent for music, and it is surprising that so little has been accomplished by them in this art. We can mention only one Spanish musician who acquired anything like eminence — Cristofano Morales, who was born at the beginning of the sixteenth century. He was admitted as a singer in the Pope's Chapel in 1540, and composed a number of masses and other pieces for the church. Escobedo and Vittoria were also good musicians, but Morales was the representative of Spanish composers.

The species of music in which the Spanish most delight is the romance; they have several beautiful compositions of this kind. The guitar is the instrument most generally employed to accompany the voice; this instrument is quite as national as their beads and their chocolate, and is to be found in every house. The Spanish guitar is constructed with double strings, each pair being tuned in unison, with the exception of the lowest, which are tuned in octaves. All play the guitar, and all have a tact in playing it. The song of the Spaniards is full of feeling; their style of music is pleasing, but variable.

CHAPTER VIII.

Germany — The Lied — Martin Luther and the Choral.

The origin of the German schools is considered to be as ancient as that of the Flemish; several German masters flourished at the same period with the French and Flemish; but the wars which devastated Germany during the latter part of the sixteenth and the beginning of the seventeenth century, and particularly the terrible *thirty years'* war, during which five great armies overran that unhappy country, carrying desolation and havoc in every part of it, — all this trial destroyed the arts, which can only flourish in the bosom of peace and happiness. It is certain that at this period the school of Germany was greatly inferior to that of Italy; it even appears that the French school began to revive before that of Germany. It seems not to have been till about the end of the seventeenth century that Germany received a marked impulse from the works of Keiser, the first German composer who, after the renovation, showed an original and superior talent.

Reinhard Keiser was born in 1673, in a little village near Leipzig. His father was a fine musician, and taught him the elements of music; and at the age of nineteen the boy was skillful in composition, and wrote the music to a pastoral. * At this period, 1692, German opera began to have a style of its own. Keiser showed great originality, and assisted much in founding the German school of operatic composition. It was in this branch of the art that Keiser gained celebrity, and for forty years he was a beloved composer. He died in 1739. (The other German masters will be mentioned in our "Biographies.")

The German *lied* † (song) is developed from the folk-song, and consists of the sacred, or choral (hymn-tune), the secular, the national (patriotic) and the humorous, styles. The German people love to sing; they sing at their work as well as at church ; and their *lied* often takes the character of a "home-song," full of pathos and honest feeling. The *choral* (hymn) originated in the reformed church of Germany. Martin Luther wrote many hymns or chorals, which were more inspiring and more vigorous than the old church music. It is the choral, indeed, that aided the

---

* A simple description of rural or country scenes.
† Pronounced *leed*.

rapid spread of those new ideas which Luther
and his earnest followers gave to the world.

Luther's relation to the music of the reformed
church was a very marked and important one.
"I wish," he said, "after the example of the
Prophets and ancient Fathers of the Church, to
make German psalms for the people; that is to
say, sacred hymns, so that the word of God may
dwell among the people by means of song also."

Luther's greatest hymn is "*Ein feste Burg ist
unser Gott*" ("A strong fortress is our God").

CHORAL.

EIN FESTE BURG IST UNSER GOTT.

M. Luther, 1529.

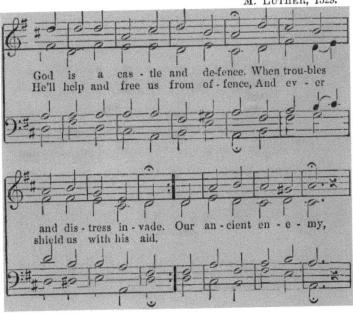

CHORAL.

By JOHANN SEBASTIAN BACH, 1703.

ear - nest is in mind, His strength he now pre-pares, With

might and sub-tle - ty; On earth is none so strong as he.

1st time p
2nd time ff

The progress of music has been steadfast and consistent in Germany, until now, in our modern times, it is at the head of all schools; indeed, German composers, since the time of Bach and Handel, seem to have produced the most important works.

Of the great German masters we shall speak in the "Biographies of Famous Musicians." (See page 61)

CHAPTER IX.

Miracle Plays — Passion Music — Oratorio.

" Miracle Plays," " Mysteries " and " Morali-
ties " were very popular throughout Europe in
the thirteenth and fourteenth centuries. They
consisted of representations of incidents and
scenes from the Holy Scriptures (such as the
life of Christ, the lives of celebrated saints, etc.),
by singing and acting. These plays did more
towards making the people familiar with the
great events of Scripture, than could have been
done by simple teaching or narrative.

The history of the Passion of our Lord became
a favorite subject in these performances ; and, as
time passed, the Passion music grew into a more
elaborate and artistic form.

The history of the Passion of our Lord has
formed part of the service for Holy Week in
every part of Christendom from time immemo-
rial ; and though, no doubt, the all-important
chapters of the Gospel in which it is contained
were originally read in the ordinary tone of

voice, without any attempt at a musical reci-tation, there is evidence enough to prove that the custom of singing it to a peculiar chant was introduced at a very early period.

Certainly, since the beginning of the thirteenth century, and probably from a much earlier period, it has been the custom to sing the music of the Passion in the following manner. The text is divided between three ecclesiastics, — called the " Deacons of the Passion,"— one of whom chants the words spoken by our Lord, another the nar-rative of the Evangelist, and the third the ex-clamations uttered by the Apostles, the crowd, and others, whose conversation is recorded in the Gospel.

Until the latter half of the sixteenth century the Passion was always sung by the three deacons alone. Still, the members of the pontifi-cal choir believed it possible to improve upon the time-honored custom ; and, in the year 1585, Vittoria produced a very simple setting of those portions of the text which are uttered by the crowd, the effect of which, intermingled with the chant sung by the deacons, was found to be so striking, that it has ever since remained in use.

The German composers in the sixteenth cen-tury began to devote attention to Passion music, and, from that time until the death of Bach, it was held in estimation.

Bach's "Passion Music," or "Passion Oratorios," are masterpieces of musical composition. In his great works the German form of *Passions Musik* reached its height; and in this it may fairly be said to have passed away; for, since the death of Bach, no one has seriously attempted, either to tread in his steps, or to strike out a new ideal fitted for this peculiar species of sacred music. The oratorio has been farther developed, and has assumed forms of which Bach could have entertained no conception; but the glory of having perfected this particular art-form remains entirely with him; and it is not at all probable that any future composer will ever attempt to rob him of his well-earned honor.

The Oratorio sprang from the Passion plays, etc., and is the highest development of sacred narrative in musical setting. It consists of airs (solos), duets, trios, choruses, recitatives, etc., musically illustrating some subject taken from the Scriptures. The word oratorio is derived from the Italian word *orare*, "to pray."

The first oratorio of which we have an account was entitled " *Rappresentazione di Anima e di Corpo.*" It was composed by Emilio del Cavaliere, and was performed and printed at Rome in 1600. It was represented in action on a stage in the church of La Vallicella, with scenes, decorations, chorus and *dances*.

The oratorio proper, however, made its appearance first in Germany not long after the beginning of the seventeenth century, and it is to that country that we are indebted for the grandest compositions of this kind. The greatest composers of oratorio music were Bach, Spohr, Handel, Haydn and Mendelssohn. (See "Biographies," page 61)

The oratorio is the highest art-form to which the musician can aspire. Very few succeed in rising to the height of musical ability necessary for the accomplishment of such a task as writing an oratorio.

Who can listen to those wonderful works, "The Messiah," by Handel, "The Creation," by Haydn, and "Elijah," by Mendelssohn, without being filled with the true spirit of devotion? Such works of art draw us nearer to the Omnipotent Power which gives to man the *genius* through which that Power speaks.

CHAPTER X.

THE OPERA.

The opera is the successor of the miracle-plays. An opera is "a dramatic entertainment, of which music is a necessary part," according to the generally accepted definition, although the word *opera* means *work*.

The Italians were the inventors of the opera; and Italy, until within a few years past, has always been considered the home of this style of music. The first opera was composed by Angelo Poliziano, and was performed at Rome in 1480. It was nothing more than a copy, slightly altered, of the "miracle-play." * It had secular (not religious) words, however, which had been prepared by Cardinal Riario.

In 1500 the Popes possessed a theatre at Rome, with scenery and mechanical contrivances; but no operatic work of consequence was produced until 1574, when Claudio Merulo composed an opera which was performed at Venice in the

* See Chapter IX.

presence of Henry III, who was passing on his way from Poland to claim the crown of France. At about the same time, Vincent Galileo, father of the great astronomer, invented the recitative, which is that part of the opera in which the words or verses are *recited* in musical tones, with no attempt at *air* or *song*. Montiverde, a musician of some fame at that time, improved the opera by giving more importance to the *accompaniment* of the singing by musical instruments.

The first opera, complete in modern form, was written by two of the best musicians of Florence, — Giulio Caccini and Giacomo Peri — in 1597.

Cherubini is said to have been the first to inaugurate the modern Italian school of opera. After him came Rossini, whose beautiful operas are so well known. Bellini, Donizetti and Verdi are also famous names among Italian composers of opera.

In France the greatest triumphs of opera were gained by Gluck, a German. The French composers who have gained celebrity, have followed his examples.

It is in Germany that the highest forms of development in the opera have been made; the expression of passion, the perfection of instrumental accompaniments, orchestral coloring and scientific writing, being especially due to German invention and influence.

In many of the German and French operas of a lighter character, spoken dialogue is introduced in the place of recitative; and the same practice is often observed in English opera, so called.

There are many varieties of opera, but the chief are : the grand opera, or *opera seria ;* the romantic opera, or *opera drammatica ;* and the comic opera, or *opera buffa.* There are of course many works which partake of more than one of the styles indicated by the above divisions; but, as a rule, these three classes are sufficiently distinct.

WHAT MUSIC
CAN DO FOR YOU

A Guide for the Uninitiated

by

HARRIET A. SEYMOUR

PREFACE

—————— to know
Rather consists in opening out a way
Whence the imprisoned splendor may escape,
Than in effecting entry for a light
Supposed to be within.

—ROBERT BROWNING.

NOW that the whole world is bent upon a constructive policy for all nations, the subject of education has become more than absorbing. Most of us have come to the conclusion that we all are in need of being re-educated. The failures of the past must become the means of leading us to a better future.

Musical re-education aims at making music a practical study for the average person by teaching him its connection with life. This is brought about by the close study of the fundamentals of hearing, and understanding what we hear. Music is a necessity; it is for all. It is "something ever singing," but it must sing consciously,

Preface

and scientifically as well as emotionally, before it becomes of educational value. It is to this end that we present this unpretentious volume to the people of America.

The author wishes to thank Miss Lieze Godwin and Miss Margaret Lee for their helpful co-operation, also those whose enthusiasm has helped to fan the flame of desire for re-education in music.

H. A. S.

WHAT MUSIC
CAN DO FOR YOU

I

AWAKENING TO LIFE THROUGH MUSIC

Musical training is a more potent instrument than any other, because rhythm and harmony find their way into the inward places of the soul, on which they mightily fasten.
—PLATO.

TO have a full life is the conscious or unconscious aim of every individual, we might say the aim of the world, for the world is nothing more than the sum total of individuals. If the consciousness of the individual is right and constructive, the world problems must of necessity adjust themselves.

By establishing harmony in the individual consciousness, harmony of mass consciousness must follow, for in the fundamental things of life individuals differ very little. The desire for more joy, more love, more health, more happiness, is universal, and makes us all akin. This life of completeness is not merely a Utopian dream; it is a practical result of co-operating with a law, the Harmonic Law.

Chaos in the world is caused by the chaos of separate lives, with their resulting actions and reactions upon other lives, and is directly due to lack of compliance with the law of Nature, that is, to the law of Harmony, for Nature is Harmony. Ignorance of Nature's law is at the bottom of all misery.

Would not every individual seek to put himself in direct accord with this law if he knew that by so doing he would make his life full and rich? Would he not do it from a purely selfish motive?

The law of Nature cannot change itself to suit the whims and ignorances of Nature's children, but it does stand ready to serve as soon as her children learn her secrets and avail themselves of them. If ignorance is the cause, the remedy is education. Not the kind we have had in the past, education in externals, but a fundamental understanding of the Harmonic Principle which governs everything in the universe, the sun and the planets, as well as each individual life. But what has this to do with music? Taught as it has been in the past, as something separate from life, it has very little to do with it, but in the new understanding, as a channel through which the law works, it has a great deal to do with it. It is the link by which the individual is made one with the law itself.

The great principle is: *First, Listening, then Thinking, and then Action.*

Start with the premise that we must formulate and carry out a new scheme of education which will be based upon the idea that man is his own salvation. In him are all the possibilities for harmony and growth. Education has only to furnish a stimulus that will cause the awakening of this larger self, thereby changing his mental images, which will in turn change his reactions and so his life.

Music will bring about this awakening; therefore in the new education it must be classed not as a luxury, but as a necessity. "It is," as Basil King says, "like water in its relation to humanity." The craving for it is apparent on all sides. Wherever there is a park concert the crowds flock to hear it. When "like the flowers that bloom in the spring, tra-la," the hurdy-gurdy comes forth from its winter of inactivity, the children gather around it to dance and sing, and the grown-up children slacken their pace as they walk by.

There is an interesting and rather touching incident that occurs every day in the Grand Central Station in New York City. In that vast arcade, which is a city in itself, there are many shops of every conceivable nature, clothing shops, candy shops, haberdasheries, restaurants, book shops, everything for the convenience and temptation of the transient population. In the midst of this hive of activity there is a little music shop where popular songs are tried out on the piano for interested purchasers. Every day at noon the stenographers and clerks from adjacent offices gather there with their lunches to spend the noon hour where they can hear a little music. For the time being the workaday world is forgotten. Cares and problems slip away, and when they go back to their offices they go back refreshed. This bit of music at the lunch hour is all that many of these girls have in their lives, and the very expression on their faces tells the story of their hunger and craving for it.

We must have music and more music. In this as in almost everything else we have two extremes. An immense gap has existed, and still exists, between those who are able to play technically well, at least, the most difficult music of the great masters, and those who, loving it more and needing it just as much, cannot afford to study. Of this latter class few can ever afford to have a piano or a phonograph in their homes.

Mankind wants peace and harmony in the world, but makes it practically impossible for the masses to have the means of attaining it. Psycho-analysts have proven conclusively that the reactions from wrong mental impressions are destructive, both to the man himself and the world in general. Take a depressed day laborer who gets up in a dirty, close room where children are crying, the mother is scolding, and the heat is overpowering. Before him is a day's work and after that a return to the same environment. Can we blame him if he becomes violent and destructive? He blames the system and we blame him, and the real truth of the matter is that neither he nor we are properly educated or this situation would not exist.

"Yes," says some one for the sake of argument, "this is all very true, but Germany has been one of the most musical countries, and surely we have had ample proof of her destructive reactions." We have, but herein lies the whole point. We must do exactly the opposite of what we have been doing. We must use music as a means to an end and not regard it as an end in itself. Music is both an art and a science. In the new order we must have vision and imagination, but we must also have an understanding of law, and learn to work out every problem according to law or principle, rather than by imagination or mere mechanical skill.

In order to enter into the spirit of music or harmony we must go back to its fundamental principle. If this method were adopted in all forms of education we should become a well-grounded nation in a most practical way. As it is we are slaves to name and form.

A man studies scientific farming, working out all sorts of elaborate problems as to cattle, milk, butter, etc., but if anything happens to the farm hand who milks the cows, he cannot get, with all his scientific knowledge, a drop of milk from the udder of the best cow alive. Take a girl who is graduated from a school of domestic science, put her into a house where there is no cook, and she will be able to tell you how many calories each person should have and what the cave man's diet was, but she will not be able to cook a decent meal.

In music a girl may have learned by imitation—that is, by having been shown over and over just how to play certain passages, to play some difficult compositions, but put her in an environment where the harmonizing of some simple tune is needed and frequently she is absolutely incapable. Her Bach and her Chopin are of no avail, for she cannot do the practical thing.

At the Music School Settlement a blind man who had been studying for a year or more complained bitterly that the teacher refused to give him what he wanted and needed. Upon investigating his case it was found that the teacher was a follower of the —— method. The blind man's desire was to be given the chords that would help him to harmonize tunes so that he might practice the songs that he had to sing in the synagogue, which meant both his outlet artistically and his means of earning a living. The teacher, however, had insisted upon his playing for an hour each day five-finger exercises of a certain type, then reading through by the Braille system for the blind a deadly dull study for the fingers, and, finally, as a great treat, playing a little "piece" fit for a child. When he came to us with his complaint the teacher grew quite irritable, explaining that he had not yet got to chords, that they did not come before volume three, and that he was only in volume one. Which is the more important, the teacher or the pupil, the method or life?

In a desire to make amends we offered to show him the three elementary chords. We felt responsible for his not having been given what he needed, so set to work to make it right. We spent two hours at the piano getting the sound of the one chord and its root, with its relation to the melody he was singing, then the four chord and then the five. His ear was already awakened, so in a short time he was able to play basses, not only to little folk songs, but also to his synagogue songs, to Schumann, Schubert, and others. The knowledge of these chords opened up harmonic consciousness in the man, curing him of his irritability and pessimism. It was also the means of securing more musical work for him, thus changing his life from one of despair to one of constructive thinking and acting.

What Music Can Do for You

To accomplish the awakening of the harmonic consciousness we must begin with music in schools. Children naturally love to sing and to skip around to lively tunes. Instead of the tedious do, re, mi method, we should begin with lovely children's songs, singing games, skipping, and dancing. In this way children are given the joyous, harmonizing atmosphere of music and are put in a musical mood before they are confronted with the mechanical and intellectual side of music.

Music is made up of melody, harmony, and rhythm. In order to enter into the essence or spirit of music one must feel and hear. After that, performance may follow if it be desired. In passing we might say that it would not hurt grown-ups to be a little more simple. We all sham too much, and musically the whole world has, so to speak, put up a bluff.

The law of melody is simple. The rhythmic swing comes first, which is different from what is termed "time," and children soon find it for themselves. Then the resting note of the tune, the center of it, or the keynote of the scale, is heard in various ways. In some children this anchorage may awaken at once; in others, not so soon. It cannot always be said when a child will become cognizant of the keynote of a tune, as many mothers and teachers would like us to do, but it is certain that they have it in them and will do so, if we have patience coupled with the right attitude. Forcing is of no avail. It has to come through naturally, and the function of the teacher is to awaken, not to instruct. After the awakening of the consciousness to harmony, melody, and rhythm instruction is possible, but not before.

To know the law and its uses, this is the eternal process. We learn to know the law of music through listening and understanding. Harmony has heretofore been taught in such a complex and external way that the average person is simply confused and gets no practical value from it. Yet how much we do need the harmonic principle for daily living!

It is indeed better for children to grow up before they are given the old-fashioned teaching, if they are to have it at all. Some mothers have known this intuitively and have allowed their children to go without music lessons rather than be given the kind of teaching which, as the children at the Settlement say, gives them "a hate on music." For this reason it is better not to have any lessons than to have mechanical, theoretical lessons: it is a kind of mentally blighting process. We spoil, by putting in the wrong idea, the music that is in the child waiting to be brought out, as, for instance, the real consciousness of God is often spoiled by the outward form of learning the prayer book by heart, learning to genu-flect, etc.

It would be better to refrain altogether until some inner religious feeling has been aroused. And so in music. Many a person's real love for music has been blighted by having first been given the outer form. They have become disgusted and their desire for music has been killed. To insist that a child shall practice every day is to find him shaking the hourglass and trying to cheat in every possible way. But give him a tune he likes to pick out and harmonize and you will have to take him away from the piano by force. This is a strong statement, but we have seen many such instances. Pupils forget to eat in their desire to find basses and tunes; others refuse to go to sleep until they have found the bass to a certain song. One mother said: "Sally doesn't come to lunch. She doesn't even hear me call her, and all on account of her absorbing interest in some little song that has caught her fancy." Another says that in order to have peace at home she is obliged to lock the piano.

The attitude of the old-time musician has been that children must grow up before studying harmony. The truth is that little children of five or six can hear the root of a chord, or "hear under," as we say, as well as, if not better than, adults. If you begin before they have been spoiled by the old external and mechanical methods of teaching, they will hear the three fundamental harmonies within themselves as easily as the birds in the woods.

The great need is, for parents, teachers,

and pupils alike, to follow the one great law of *listening first*, then action. Quite naturally you ask what we mean by listening. It is just this. To sit quietly and when perfectly relaxed, mentally and physically, repeat some phrase or verse, such as:

"He prayeth best who loveth best
All things both great and small."

Get the swing, the rhythm, or rhyme of these words; it will come to you from the idea or sense of the words. In this instance the importance is easily found to rest on the words, *prayeth, loveth, things, great and small*. The swing, then, is out on *prayeth*, in on *loveth*, out on *things*, in on *great and small*. Now quietly listen for a tune, to the first phrase of the verse, "He prayeth best. . . . " The tune will come naturally when the rhythm is grasped. Any child easily hears a tune to words and will respond almost instantly, and adults can do the same thing if they will let go of self-consciousness. These tunes come without effort from children of all ages. Here are two examples, the first from a boy of seven who had never had a music lesson.

Oh how I love the sum - mer time!

And this from a girl of eleven who had had the kind of lessons that had made her hate music.

How would you like to go up in a swing?

Music—that is, melody, harmony, and rhythm—is inherent in everybody, only waiting to be brought out. By that we do not mean that everyone can be a Beethoven, but that everyone has some music, some connecting link with melody and harmony within him. Music gives an unlimited chance to develop this inner sense, making it grow, as does a plant, first underground, unseen and unheard, then visibly.

All studies should be based upon this law—from within, out, and mathematics and music should come first on the list.

Mathematics is so closely allied to music that it is an intensely interesting thing to follow. There are seven tones to a scale. These tones are related through mathematical vibration. There are three chords, all resolving into one. The twenty-four keys of music are found to bear the same relationship to one another as the chords to one another—that is, the next sharp key is five up, the next flat key is four up. One, four, five are the three elementary chords. A circle of keys works out perfectly and the three chords form a triangle as , and so on up to higher mathematics and into overtones and the fourth dimension.

The following incident illustrates the awakening which comes through listening. A young girl had become unhappy and pessimistic through the study of social conditions in their chaotic state. Music teachers in Europe and in this country advised her to practice more, but no amount of practice brought relief to her troubled mind. Finally one of the new music teachers tried to persuade her that

law does exist and reign, that man is his
own salvation, but she remained uncon-
vinced—when suddenly the teacher played
the scale down, leaving off the last note,
and the girl involuntarily sang it.

"Where did that come from?" asked the
teacher.

"I heard it inside," answered the girl.
"You are right. There is a law and it's
in me."

After listening quietly and hearing inwardly there comes an inner sense of harmony. The chaos of vagrant thoughts is
calmed into repose; the mind is stilled to
outside influences and becomes a reflector
for the inner light which comes only
through stillness. Thoughts become positive, ideas are born, and one dares to dream
of great accomplishments, and through the
stillness comes the thought, "I can and I
will." Those things which seemed beyond
reach come quite naturally within the realm
of possibility. Faith in our own powers is
built up when the chaotic thoughts of the
outside world are stilled, and we believe
in our own ability to be and to do what we

will. Dreams and ideals which have been vague take on definite form, shaping themselves under the influence of that harmony which has been established through listening.

II

MELODY, RHYTHM, AND HARMONY

In no other study is performance so insisted upon.
—DALCROZE.

BY the New Education we mean that we are to begin by recognizing the potential possibilities of every child and seek to draw these out. Education no longer means filling a void, but developing that which is latent in the individual. We are to be continually constructive in spite of the fact that we are bound to be discriminating; idealistic, but at the same time practical. We are to seek to find in everyone the germ, at least, of the hidden talent that formerly we did not trouble ourselves about unless it gave marked evidences of its existence.

With these ideas well fixed in mind let

us see how they can best be applied to music. First let us consider what music is and what angles of approach it offers. As an art, music is a symbol of the art of life. It has as its mainspring the same source— God. As a science it belongs to that branch known as mathematics, numbers, whose underlying principle is order. It has yet another angle, one which depends upon the recognition of both the former ones. It is a language—the greatest of all languages, since it can say that which no words can ever convey. To understand this universal language, to intensify it and so enrich our lives, is the object of music-teaching under the new educational system. We want music to be of practical use to everyone, and to make it that we must cease imitating and get down to fundamentals.

In the old method it was necessary for the pupil to depend eternally upon the teacher, so in most cases he grew bored and ceased to play at all. No one can remain really interested in a subject for any length of time unless there is a possibility of getting something to work out alone. But if one begins with hearing the principles of melody, rhythm and harmony can then be learned, and from these one can always advance alone into a larger and larger understanding.

With this hearing knowledge of melody, rhythm, and harmony, music becomes more "usable." A boy or girl is enabled to play an accompaniment in any key for the fun of a sing after dinner, a mother can turn home into a real heaven by playing songs for her children. She can play dances, too, and without having to search the piano for the notes of that "skippy dance" that the children like so much. She may not play Beethoven's fifty-one variations, and yet she may, according to the interest she has in learning the more difficult compositions of the masters. But the point is that she can do something with music which has practical value and will lend grace and harmony to life. But to do this we must begin at the very beginning.

We are coming to realize that in almost everything a certain vanity of being "advanced" has led us to skip the fundamentals. Everyone wants to do the fourth year's work in the first year! But we can get real enjoyment and interest out of foundation building. To hear inwardly a simple tune and its harmonies is worth more than to *play* a concerto without consciously hearing a single note of it. Being really musical means to hear inwardly, and the new education in music aims to awaken this inner musical consciousness.

Once this sense is awakened music becomes a practical help in education. It develops the power of concentration, in that one is forced to do the work himself. No one can hear for you, no matter how good a teacher he may be. It awakens what some one has so aptly termed the "submerged self," which brings about the inward development toward which all education is directed. In other words, it is a great freeing process, a practical means of awakening a sense of love, law, and order-the trinity of all freedom.

So music takes on a new aspect. It is no longer a mere accomplishment, it is a psychological means of liberation, a vital necessity to us all, and a practical educational subject which we can no longer afford to neglect. But to make use of its value we must change our method of attack.

Music is primarily a language of sound, and it is this sound, and sequence of sounds, that is of value to us. We must learn to capture a melody with our inner ear, hear it not only as a melody, that, is, with the relation of one note to the other, but as rhythm and as harmony. This requires that we feel, think, and finally analyze; then that we rehearse our feeling, utilizing what thought and analysis have contributed. But what is to be gained by this? Let us be practical.

Suppose, for example, that something in your life is troubling you, that some one whom you love is in dire distress or that your own personal affairs are in such a muddle that you can see no way out. You are growing ill, going round and round in a circle of fears from which you are unable to escape. In desperation you go to hear some music, hoping to forget for a moment.

What Music Can Do for You

As the orchestra plays the strains of a Beethoven symphony or some lovely modern tone poem you find your nervous tension loosening. Your mind pauses, so to speak, to listen to the sweetness, the power of the sound. You are released from the paralysis of fear, and suddenly a way out presents itself, a simple solution which you were too tense to see before the music loosened you.

Now suppose that by studying the fundamentals of music from the listening side only you were enabled, without attending a concert, to recall this feeling at will; you would then be in a position to utilize one of the greatest powers of music. You could seat yourself in your own room and inwardly repeat all that lifted you above your worries. You would have within you the necessary technique for solving problems, for quieting your nerves, and for resting your body. For it is through the awakening of melody, rhythm, and harmony in our minds that we are able to express these self-same things in our bodies and in our affairs.

But to obtain this useful technique we must apply ourselves diligently to each of the three elements of music. Melody is the most obvious of the three, rhythm the most primitive, and harmony the least understood.

When a Beethoven hears a melody he does not hear it as a thing separate and distinct in itself, he hears not only the tune, but its rhythm and harmony as well. He hears the three things as one. Oneness, unity, is the big underlying law. There is only one supreme chord, the tonic into which all the others must resolve, just as there is but one solution to all problems—oneness with God.

But there are steps to be taken before we, who are continually seeing our separateness, can achieve the creative awakening which will bring us to the same sense of oneness with melody, rhythm, and harmony that Beethoven had. Music was his natural element; all things spoke to him in its terms. As he walked abroad the woods, the flowers, the brooks, the birds all contributed their part to the motifs which are still inspiring, helping, and healing humanity to-day. He had brought with him a fully awakened musical consciousness which enabled him to hear that which we

unawakened ones do not—tne music of the
spheres, a continuous, glorious symphony.
Why, most of us cannot follow a simple
folk song, swing its rhythm, or find its bass!
How then can we possibly expect to enter
into the consciousness of Beethoven?

Yet it can be accomplished, and the reward is in far greater proportion than that
of many studies which heretofore have been
considered of indispensable value.

Music understood from the hearing side,
studied through listening, thinking, and
feeling, brings us closer to truth, to an understanding of ourselves and a harmonization of conditions, than any other study.
A noted sociologist, who openly goes to
war with "art for art's sake," says that to
her music and life are so closely interwoven
that a single term should suffice for both.
And it is for this that we are aiming—to
make a conscious union between our life and
music. To do this we must study each of
the elements of music with a view to
finding each within ourselves and bringing
them into a perfect union through intelligent listening and feeling.

III

MELODY

A tune is a spiritual thing.—SCHUMANN.

NOTHING repays so well in any study as getting down to an understanding of the simple law of things and working it out step by step until we actually have it or become one with it. "Some people think they know, some know, and some know that they know."

In music, as in other sciences, we must *know* that we *know* in order to enter completely into its spirit.

We are living in an age of scientific analysis, where every thought, act, and emotion is being subjected to the X-ray of comprehensive research. The war has brought us up with a sharp turn and made us face ourselves more frankly. We want to be sure that what we are spending, whether it is time or money, is spent intelligently. Granting this, it is an interesting and significant fact that during the worst phases of the war, when rich and poor alike were counting every penny, people flocked to concerts. There was "standing room only" an hour before the music began. People seemed to hunger and thirst for it.

But why does the average person go to a concert, and what does he get out of it? Often not even a tune to carry away. Most commonly it is merely a certain emotional exaltation. But a purely emotional and sentimental reaction will not enable the hearer to appropriate for permanent use his sensations of pleasure and delight, and he therefore fails to get the amount of mental poise, the physical relaxation, and the true spiritual significance that he would get if he heard understandingly and etched what he heard on his memory, to be recalled and reimaged at will.

Music is generally accepted as a softening, harmonizing influence, necessary to all people. From the hospital ward to the concert hall the cry is for more music. But out of the thousands who buy tickets for a concert, how many get more than a passing wave of pleasant sound?

It is an interesting experiment to choose an ordinary group of people and try them out musically in simple ways. For example, suppose your group to have just heard a concert, such as one of the New York Symphony concerts, the program consisting of the Dvorak "New World Symphony," some songs, and perhaps the "Symphonic Poem" of Liszt. Take the first motif of the "New World Symphony," which is really a simple folk tune, and ask

any of your group if they can hum that tune. If they can, ask them to draw in lines a picture of the direction the melody takes—to make "a pitch picture." The idea is, that if the realm of music is to be entered through *hearing* one must begin by being able to follow the tune through its pitch.

What Music Can Do for You

A very intelligent man who goes to many concerts every year once told me that it was impossible for him to tell which direction the tune of "Three Blind Mice" takes, and that he had given up trying to hear more because his professional friends had been so discouraging and superior. Most people are deaf to melody, but by training the ear through the inner process of listening, it becomes an easy and natural thing to follow a tune correctly.

If thoughts are things, and they are, musical thoughts, in the sense of tunes that we can hear within, are an addition to the general good and are conducive to peace and harmony both individually and nationally. It seems extravagant to claim that, if everyone could be shown how to follow a tune and to remember it, the world's unrest would be ameliorated, but this would seem to be a fact, nevertheless. Because, by so doing, each individual would become conscious of the harmony within himself and would express that harmony to an extent varying according to the degree of its awakening.

Melody

Psycho-analysts claim that physical ailments are caused by destructive mental impressions. Since mental impressions rehearsed make up the sum total of human consciousness, it is therefore worth our while to learn consciously to follow the melody line of a beautiful motif and to register and keep it. This would result in something more permanent than a mere temporary sensation of pleasure, as we shall prove.

A young man, well educated, ordinarily strong, with devoted friends and plenty of money, became unhappy and discouraged as the result of illness. He decided that there was nothing worth while in life for him, so concluded to let go and die. The doctor had told him that if he did let go, that unless he put up a fight for life, he would die. As he lay, contemplating death, the memory of the second movement of Beethoven's immortal Fifth floated through his mind:

Beethoven.   Vth Symphony.

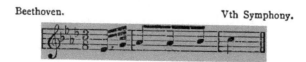

What Music Can Do for You

He listened to the subjective concert
with joy in his heart, which came from the
fact that he could hear and register a tune.
He became more and more absorbed in it,
imbued with its harmony and, through it,
he was stirred to a desire for life and its
fullness, and with a supreme effort put up
the fight which brought about his recovery.
He is now a valuable citizen and has since
become a powerful instrument for the
strength of the Allied cause and for peace.

Music has been studied by the so-called
talented people in a complex, expensive, and
too often egotistical way. Counterpoint
and fugue may be all right for such as
these, but for the average person who goes
to concerts something much more simple is
needed, and, if the truth be told, a great
many of these musically educated ones are
lacking in an understanding of simple
fundamentals.

It is better to enter into the spirit of a
melody by really hearing it than to play
a complex composition in a purely external
way, for "Music is harmony, harmony is
love, and love is God," said Sidney Lanier.

Melody

That great clergyman, Heber Newton, who courageously went ahead of his time in so many ways, and with whom, happily, the times have now caught up, gives us the following in his *Mysticism and Music:*

A scientific musician bethought him of making the chords of music record the lines of their sound waves so that the eye could have a picture of the forms thus produced. Suspending five pens from the wires of a piano so that they should move delicately over sheets of paper, by striking the chords carefully and allowing the sound to die out naturally, he succeeded in making the vibrations of the sound waves of each chord trace the lines of its movements.

The results were designs of mathematical exactness of exquisite beauty, strangely suggesting the great typical flower forms. These diagrams were thus the expression to the eye of the music which the ear hears, the audible world translated into the visible world, the revelation of a mystery until then unseen by human eye, ungrasped by human thought.

Music is a language, although it is really something more. It might be termed the universal language, one to which all nationalities and races respond. In the same sense it is a religion, symbolizing the Oneness or Love which unites all people.

What Music Can Do for You

The Sufi religion, one of the cults of India, is based on sound, and their claim is that sound—that is, music—will bring us closer to what is termed God-consciousness, or Universal Love, than any other medium.

We have all had the experience of being lifted out of petty worries and selfish desires through some wonderful music, especially singing, like the Russian choir, a fine string quartet, or an orchestra. Therefore, realizing the power of music, is it not worth while to put ourselves consciously into the spirit of music that we may understand its message? Let us hear it silently, listen to it, understand it, then, remembering it through this understanding, act upon it. So will the action which follows always be a melody in itself.

Now what is melody? It is a definite idea expressed in a sequence of sounds, producing a unified impression. It is the golden thread which runs through all music, forming what we call the tune or air. It can be likened to the plot of a story, where setting, environment, and action all revolve around the main idea; or to the theme of a poem.

In the language of words it is like making the short statement, "I love you," and repeating it in various inflections of the voice, then elaborating this statement by telling what awakens this love—blue eyes, sunny smile, beautiful nature, etc.—and then coming back to the original theme, "I love you."

Musicians use the terms "motif" and "phrase," which are very simple terms to understand. Motif is the smallest pattern of the melody. Music has distinct patterns, and in this respect we can go back to nature and find, in form, the same plan that exists in relation to sound. Flowers, snowflakes, stars, moon, sun, all have a few simple forms which occur over and over again.

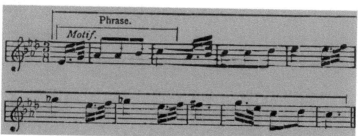

Sound has form, and melody creates itself from very simple patterns, elaborated and repeated in different keys, just as the triangle, the circle, and the square repeat themselves and combine in nature, thus creating other more complex forms. Motif is, then, the smallest pattern in music. In "Three Blind Mice" the motif or smallest pattern is

This little pattern of three notes is repeated and then repeated again, from a higher spot, and then elaborated and repeated again.

A phrase is a more complete musical thought, ending either in what we may call a comma or a period. We are too prone to juggle terms without the slightest idea of their meaning. Teachers who understand the meaning of certain technical phrases too often take it for granted that the pupil also understands. A teacher once asked a little girl the definition of the word "phrase," meaning, of course, in a musical sense. The child thought a moment and then said in an exultant tone of voice, "It is the French word for straw-berry."

Another little story, which is amusing as well as indicative of the lack of under-standing of the simplest things, is of the little girl who went home after a music lesson and asked her mother how many carrots there are in a bushel, explaining that her music teacher had asked her this same question. Mystified, the mother asked the teacher what carrots and bushels had to do with music. The teacher, equally mystified, thought over the questions of the day before and finally exclaimed, "Why, the question I asked was, 'How many beats are there to a measure'?" Do not these examples serve as a commentary on all education?

To enter into the real sense of a phrase, both spiritually and intellectually, we must first get the motif of the melody, then look for the place where we should naturally breathe if we were singing it (and it can be done much better if it is sung), and then find the place where we should naturally stop. In this way you have the principle of melody. It has pattern or form, it has pitch, and it says something, which is punctuated just as any other language is punctuated.

The pattern of a tune is most easily explained by illustrations. The idea is that the line of sound varies just as the line in a drawing, or of a tree, or a hillside, varies. It has an upward trend, a downward trend, or it travels along on a straight line.

People who have never paid attention to melody in the sense of being able to really hear it, and so making it their own for all time by becoming conscious of it, are surprised when they discover themselves unable to say whether "The Star-spangled Banner" moves from above downward or from below upward. It is so simple that no one realizes how dimly he hears until it is pointed out to him. Now here is a pitch picture of the beginning of "The Star-spangled Banner":

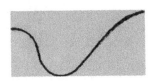

In other words, a pitch picture is the line which the tune describes. Here is a picture of "Drink to Me Only with Thine Eyes."

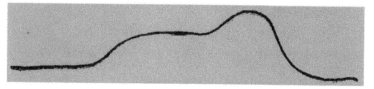

This may seem a little complicated and an easier way is to make little dots like this:

In fact, each person may work out a way of his own so long as the same principle is there.

Here is an illustration of the last tune written out in notes with the line following it:

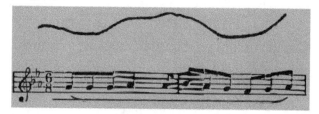

Then to be added to this are duration pictures, little lines which would show whether the sounds we hear are long or short. These help us to make rapid sketches to aid our memories. Here is a duration picture of "Over There":

Here is one of "Smiles":

It is a case of inwardly following the tune and noting the length of the different sounds. By combining the duration and the pitch pictures one gets a clue to the tune which will recall it. Of course musicians do this naturally, but the general public has been shut out from the real benefits of music through having no simple way of taking a musical short hand.

A musical friend of ours had been off in the wilds for a long time. She returned to New York just in time to hear a great violinist play the Beethoven violin concerto in the key of G. She was entranced by it, and in order to register it in her mind, thereby having it always for her own, she jotted down on the program this picture of the motif of the last movement.

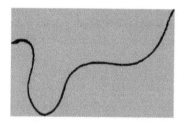

So, instead of its being merely a fleeting pleasure, that wonderful, inspired melody became at once a part of her. She was conscious of it in its elements of pitch and duration, and could recall it to memory whenever she desired.

Here the phonograph is of real help. We can play a tune over and over, making pitch pictures and duration pictures until we become so adept that the concert hall holds no terrors for us.

The majority of us have only sensations where we should have experiences—vivid, clear, easily recalled, and reimaged experiences—with which we may change the dark times of fear and worry into times of beauty, harmony, and peace. This is truly the function of music, but we cannot have this power without paying the price of a little time and attention.

IV

RHYTHM

> Amid the mysteries that become more mysterious the more they are thought about, there will remain the one absolute certainty, that we are ever in the presence of an infinite and eternal energy, from which all things proceed.
> —HERBERT SPENCER.

IMAGINE the world without rhythm and perhaps you can get some conception of what rhythm really is. Every great teacher has virtually said that God is all; that all else is delusion, unreality, nothing. Even the man who says that all is matter simply uses another term for the same thing. The idea remains that everything in the universe is composed of one substance, the term we use to designate this substance is unimportant, be it God, Matter, Light, or what not.

We are told by scientists that everything is in vibration. The form a thing will take depends upon its rate of vibration. Wood is vibration at one rate, light is vibration at another; the difference between a hod carrier and a seer is the difference in their rates of vibration. Now rhythm is vibration slowed down sufficiently for us to realize it—a more exact definition than that, it is almost impossible to give; but the most satisfactory way of getting an understanding of it is to look for it in nature, and to learn about it in that way. This will lead you to recognize that there are large rhythms and small rhythms, wheels within wheels, so to speak. The big rhythms are the celestial bodies in their swing out and back, the seasons, the sun, the tides, etc. Inside of the big rhythms we find smaller ones; the year has a natural division of seasons, the twenty-four hours, divided into day and night, an out swing and a back swing, like the pendulum of a clock, and yet there is only one swing—the eternal underlying swing of the universe. Nature has been showing us this law for æons and we can apply its principle to music just as well as to anything else.

Rhythm

Rhythm points eternally tc unity in diversity. It is better to begin our study by actually swinging such rhythms as we can. "Do the thing and the power comes." So let us seek some simple, practical ways of coming into the realization of rhythm in music.

A great confusion between rhythm and "time" exists in the minds of most people. The simplest way of experiencing the fact of the big rhythmic swing, underlying all music, is to get some one to play all sorts of familiar things to you, and for you to swing your arm as you feel, for example, to the tune "Dixie":

you would swing up until you came to C, and then down.

To "London Bridge is falling down" the

up swing would last until G, and then the down swing would come, ending on C.

A phonograph will help very much in swinging rhythms by yourself. Folk music and dances are good for this sort of thing. People are generally quite surprised to find that the "Blue Danube Waltz" swings up and back, when they always thought of it as in *three* time.

The big swing gives a fundamental sense of rhythm which is far more useful than counting.

Children taught in this way, even those who appear to have little or no sense of rhythm, get such a really awakened rhythmic sense that when they go to school they are picked out for the way they dance. The sense of rhythm is potential in every one, but in a great many people it has never been awakened. Sometimes people who

play very well, but are nervous, lose their
nervousness through inwardly realizing the
rhythmic swing while they are playing. Several such cases have come to our notice,
and concentration upon rhythm, as a swing
out and back, has a steadying influence
upon the mind.

To be able to feel the rhythm of something
to which one is listening makes us more
conscious, thereby giving us a better
idea of what the composer felt during his
contract with the inner world of beauty,
whose messages he is delivering to us.
Counting sometimes, indeed very often,
blocks rhythm. Time is inside of rhythm.
It is the mechanical means of determining
time. In the "Blue Danube Waltz," for instance, the time is 1 2 3—the rhythm is 2.

To sing a tune, and at the same time to
swing its rhythm, is a good way of learning
to feel it. Dalcroze has a complete system
of what he calls Eurhythmics. Even for

ordinary people who have no time to spend in special studies, some of his ideas are a help. For instance, take the "Blue Danube," and swing the big rhythm while you step the time. Swing one, two, and step 1 2 3. A whole family could easily grow rhythmically conscious by spending an hour or so in the evening working out these fundamental ideas. Of course there are complexities of rhythm, but these are unnecessary to the average person, and at all events it is better to grow fundamentally rhythmic before trying the complex.

The word "rhythm" is sometimes defined as "proportion." It is certain that there must be pulsation—or motion—with a sense of more rest in one spot than in another, or more importance in one spot than in another. People call this "accent," but this seems a dangerous word, because it often leads to such terrible playing. People should not put an "accent" on the first note of every measure. It is like reciting poetry with jerky emphasis on each important word. Music flows; it does not come in hunks. When a great master is inspired to write a song or a symphony he does not hear a regularly accented string of notes: he hears a musical phrase which says something. Take the lines,

"He prayeth best who loveth best,
All things both great and small."

Say them with a strong accent on prayeth and loveth, and you have that unpleasant jerkiness which is not beautiful. It is the same in music. People often play in "bars," as they call it. In fact, people very often practice in bars. A violinist once rejoiced that he had "gotten outside of bars, at last," meaning that he had been able to hear a musical phrase *as* a phrase and not as lumps of sound. It is really a pity that music has to be written with bar lines, and people ought to try to think of music in phrases, just as they would poetry. This takes away the dull, unrhythmic quality which so many people have painfully acquired by counting in bars instead of singing in phrases. For advanced students harmony and rhythm are closely linked, and the harmony colors the rhythm, one might say. But this is, as Kipling says, another story. Suffice it to say, swing the big rhythm—to musical phrases—and you will become more and more rhythmically conscious. Your body will respond in health and your mind in happiness.

V

HARMONY

What is it to be really musical? When you have music in your heart and head.—SCHUMANN.

THE great need of the world to-day is harmony. We all realize that something is wrong and are ready to try some new way. But everyone will agree that there must be a state of repose before anything constructive can take root. Can music contribute practically to bringing about this state?

In a preceding chapter we dealt with the various possibilities of melody and rhythm in relation to general, as well as musical, education, and we hope that the reader now realizes that there is a definite value to be obtained from a better understanding of music. To achieve not only this better understanding, but to make music a component part of our lives, we must make each of its three elements our own. We must be able to use not only melody and rhythm, but harmony as well. As we have only to add the harmonies to find greater beauties in a melody, so we have but to come into harmony with life to see its fuller beauties and possibilities.

Now the harmony of music and the harmony of life both have for their foundation the same law—the law of order. Harmony in music is not the intricate study that we have been led to believe, speaking quite simply. It is the law of order as applied to music. Take, for example, two chords; one clashes and jars, giving one the sense of unrest, while the other gives the ear and mind a sense of repose. All the elements of harmony are in both, and when we have used the principles of harmony the first will resolve itself into the second and be transformed. For in reality there is only one chord, just as there is only one God. All the other chords are moving toward this one chord, just as we mortals are all

moving toward a realization of our oneness
with God.   There are, in other words, many
elements, which taken separately are un-
harmonic, but when brought into the
proper order by the application of the law,
resolve into one Great Harmony.

So it is with life.   If in our imaginations,
our minds, we could see people as harmonic
in thought, word, and deed, that is, all
striving, however discordantly, to attain
some kind of harmony with life, we would
do much to bring about the very state of
repose for which the whole world longs.
But we must do even more than this.   We
must bring harmony as an active force into
their lives, and what better way is there of
accomplishing this than through the language that everyone loves—music?

We know any number of people who have
changed all sorts of difficult conditions in
their lives either through the study of music
or by the harmonic principle in life becoming
apparent to them through music.   A young
girl, to give a definite and personal experience, who complained bitterly of pov-
erty, ill health, disappointment, and unkind

treatment of friends came to us for help. At first it seemed almost hopeless, because she would not face herself, but one day a rift was found in her armor which made her see that the only logical way of interpreting life is to know that the outside is but the reflection of the inside; that if there was a lack of harmony in her objective, external life there was something wrong in her. From that time she gradually developed strength of character enough to face herself. One by one she overcame the dragons of fear, envy, laziness, worry, and self-pity that had blocked her progress, and grew into a splendid, strong, happy, healthy, and self-reliant woman, who not only supports herself comfortably, but is able to volunteer a great deal of time to developing harmony in others.

Then we knew a boy whose life had been much handicapped by stuttering, and who had quarreled with his father, who suddenly awoke to the symbolism of music, through harmonizing tunes. He knocked timidly at my door, drew close to me and whispered: "What is this? I feel that life is changed.

I can talk without stuttering and my father came and put his arm around me and brought me home. Now I believe I can have anything I want." Later he was sent to a university and educated for the profession he had dreamed of.

Another girl was handicapped, apparently, by the most distressing home conditions—a drunken father, a sick mother, and a lazy streak in herself. Once awake to the possibilities of the harmonic law, she worked unceasingly with herself, doing everything, on the material plane as well as on the mental and spiritual, to harmonize every dissonance. In a few years she had moved her family into a better apartment, had given her mother the nourishing food and fresh air that would restore her health, and had deported the drunken father to an environment which better suited his unharmonized consciousness.

Harmony is not a passive thing; it is active and alive and as contagious as the measles. But the law works both ways; just as one bad apple in a barrel will spoil all the rest, so will an inharmonious person create an atmosphere which will communicate itself to everyone who comes within his reach. Like the inkfish which is armed with a pouch full of inky fluid for the purpose of blinding its enemies, how easily a depressed person casts an inky gloom around a room! On the other hand, one person who is in tune will harmonize a whole family without saying a word. How quickly a jolly and well-harmonized person will bring up the tone of that same group of people! We can all tune up every thought, word, and deed. Tune up our own instruments that we may each take our place in the great orchestra which plays the symphony of life.

Most people imagine, on hearing the word "harmony" in relation to the study of music, that it implies long years of dry plodding. Such has too often been the case, but is no longer so. Anyone can be taught through listening to recognize the simple harmonies of a tune, and everyone should be taught. For, when the law of harmony is embodied in the cellular structure of our bodies, its outer expression is health and peace. Health, mental and physical, should always be our first consideration, since no great heights can be attained without it. So, if listening understandingly will help to bring about peace and health, we have within our grasp not only our development in the art of music, but through it our development in life.

To make this effective there is a simple musical training which will wake in us our latent harmonic consciousness. This in turn will give us a practical knowledge of harmony in music and arouse in us a corresponding vibration in our bodies and lives.

Given a tune, the object is to be able to hear its harmonic setting. Negroes and South Sea Islanders can do this without training. Children unspoiled by mechanical training can "hear under"—that is, hear naturally the underlying harmonies of a melody. At the Music School Settlement in New York we have tested hundreds of children, and only about three out of every hundred are unable to hear and sing the fundamental harmonies. So we find that the three harmonies are potentially present in everyone. God is no respecter of persons, and harmony is the gift of God. But it remains for us, having found it in ourselves, to accept the gift and use it for our own development and the betterment of the world.

The first step for one who desires this harmonic education is to hear the keynote. That music means more when the keynote is heard is quite natural when one realizes that it is in this way that the inner realm of harmony is consciously contacted. We grope around in darkness, seeking peace, rest, and quiet, quarreling with life and everyone about us because we do not achieve satisfaction, when right in our very midst is the path to the sun which will illumine us.

"Ye have eyes and see not, ears have ye and ye hear not." It is these unhearing ears and unseeing eyes that have been the cause of our inharmony. But, through the proper understanding of music, hearing ears and seeing eyes will be developed, opening up new worlds of sound and sight within us. For these faculties are given us as tools, and through their right use we can here and now bring about for ourselves infinitely better, happier, and fuller lives. Too many people say, "When I make enough money I shall retire and take up music as an amusement." That is putting the cart before the horse. Since fullness of life is that which everyone desires, why put off until the end of life the study which would accomplish this purpose? Why not turn about and get a knowledge of the law of harmony which would increase a thousandfold the consciousness and appreciation of life, love, and truth?

A great many people, especially men and boys, probably because their voices lie low, often play good basses to college songs, hymns, etc. It is natural to them, but the trouble is that they do this unconsciously. Now we, as human beings, are above the animals in point of evolution; we have the power to do what we do consciously and with reason rather than by instinct. We have the ability to mentally rehearse an experience, thus registering the image upon the brain. Therefore, if these basses are played consciously and understandingly, the whole principle of harmony will be understood and become of practical use.

As with everything else, we must begin at the beginning. We too often build without a proper foundation, thereby only cheating ourselves; nor does this apply alone to the lay musician. A great many accomplished performers and teachers have done the same thing. They can play a Chopin scherzo, but ask them to play "'Way Down upon the Suwanee River" and they are lost. They cannot do it without notes.

How curious it is that we have gone on all these years deluding and fooling ourselves into thinking that performing a few easily forgotten "pieces" is knowing music! If anything in life is not of practical, everyday use, what good is it? Music should not be a thing apart from the rest of life. We must hear inwardly in order to have a better outward life. We must understand melody, harmony, and rhythm really to enter into the realization of music; to so find harmony, beauty, and serenity within ourselves, and from that center change our characters and life conditions.

In looking at pictures we get the effects of outline and color by knowing an angle from a curve, and being able to distinguish red from yellow; it is much the same in music. We enter into the spirit of music by intellligently hearing from within the direction which the melody takes, its rhythm, the keynote, and the fundamental chords underlying it. There are three chords, the eternal triangle, always resolving into one. Anyone can learn to inwardly hear these chords under a melody. The first step is the right attitude of mind— that is, faith and confidence in the power to hear, and this is dependent upon mental and physical relaxation. To become relaxed and still, requires a certain technique and discipline. It does not take long for the average person to accomplish this, but, like everything else, it differs with the individual. The easiest way to relax is to repeat some verse or words that present the idea of quiet to the mind and the body.

Having become as relaxed as possible, play

a scale downward, beginning on C. When you have played seven notes pause and analyze your feeling. It will be one of unrest, incompleteness. Add an eighth note, another C, and the resulting feeling will be one of rest, completion. Repeat this exercise, only vary it a trifle by playing the scale upward. Here you will find the same feeling of incompletion until you add the final C. Try this in other scales and the effect will always be the same, so perforce we learn that the law of order demands that all sounds, notes, progress either downward toward the first note or sound, or upward to a repetition of the first note, the eighth of the scale. Having found that this is true in the simplest of all tunes, see if it is not equally true in the folk song and other simple airs. Now this note from which all the other notes proceed and return is called the keynote. It is an astonishing fact that two-thirds of the people who play are unconscious of the key in which they are playing. Key in music is like home in life: it is the resting place, the note that receives, we might say, all of the others and to which they all go quite naturally. It is from this note that the piece, be it song, sonata, or symphony, gets its signature. We say a sonata is in F if its keynote is F, or in A if its keynote is A, or in D if its keynote is D.

Sing "Tramp, Tramp, Tramp, the Boys Are Marching," and stop here:

Ask yourself whether you have landed on a note that gives a sense of completion. No? Then go on until you do, and it will be:

This is the keynote.

Having trained yourself by singing the keynote of innumerable songs, etc., you are then in a position to go farther. Since you have already established the keynote of "Tramp, Tramp, Tramp, the Boys Are Marching," let us continue with that song.

Sing over the first phrase slowly. Listen attentively and try to hear the first underlying chord. Do not feel around on the piano for it; wait until you have *heard* it within, then play it. Having found the first harmony, the first chord, which in this case would be

that is the I chord based on the keynote, which is C. (We have chosen the key of C because to most people it is the easiest of keys, but any key will do as well.) Now sing the next phrase and see if you hear a like harmony; failing to do so, continue until you do. Having firmly established this chord in your consciousness, return to the beginning and commence a new search for a new harmony. This harmony will be

the V chord whose base or root note is the fifth of the scale, or G. This chord is a restless chord, it can never stay put, but must move up or down, one way or the other, and the law of harmony demands that it resolve itself into the I chord, so we have

A new harmony now presents itself and we hear

the IV chord built on the fourth of the
scale, F, which, though not so determinedly
restless as V, still must resolve back to the
I chord, as you will *hear* in the last phrase.

These are the three fundamental chords
that you must seek to hear under every
melody that comes to your ears. Thoroughly to familiarize yourself with them,
reverse the exercise and instead of singing
the melody, waiting until you hear the
harmony and then playing it, play the
melody, wait until you are conscious of the
harmony, then sing its root note, the note
on which the two upper notes stand.
Having sung this, sing the two remaining
notes of the chord.

Harmony

If you will continue this practice faithfully over a few weeks, you will gradually wake within yourself that source of harmony and peace that will draw everything in your life into its proper relation, as well as enable you to harmonize simple tunes.

So you come to hear the three fundamental chords that are all in reality that there is to harmony. The rest are merged chords, blended out of these three fundamentals, just as we blend colors. If you know the three primary colors, red, yellow, and blue, you have the key to all the rest. Knowing the principle or law of any subject gives you the power of working out every possible problem connected with that subject.

In this way we get at the inside or truth of music. One word to remember is "wait." If you are listening for the keynote, relax and wait until you hear it. Do not think. This listening is deeper than thought. It is feeling.

If you want to hear the keynote, give yourself part of a tune, then in silence and peaceful expectation wait until your inner ear reports that note to you. This process is a much more natural one than we think. There is nothing mysterious about it. We are each one of us a part of the whole, therefore why should we not, by realizing a certain quietness and oneness with that whole, be given the answer to any question? A drop of water partakes of all the qualities of an immense reservoir, then why should we not partake of all the qualities of the universal life?

This brings us to the consideration of two other parts of harmony. The first is what is known as "mode"—that is, the music you are playing in the minor mode or the major. Again it is a question of listening. Play the chord of C (C, E, G), change the middle note to E flat, then play these chords again, first one, then the other, trying to analyze the feeling they give you. C, E, G is in the major mode, C, E flat, G is in the minor. People sometimes say that the minor is sad, and it is true that all funeral marches are written in the minor mode. But there are a number of compositions written in the minor mode which are not sad, such as "The Wild Horseman" of Schumann and "The Album Leaf" of Grieg. Still, specialists in folk music maintain that oppressed people always express themselves in the minor mode.

All children do not by *any means* feel the minor to be sad. If you play these two chords to a child, asking what difference he finds, he may answer you in the terms of color. Some say that the minor is "deeper." One seven-year-old child, when hearing the minor chord for the first time, said, "I am alone in a desert."

Bach usually ended a composition with a major chord, even though he had written the whole of it in the minor, thereby conveying the idea that he considered the minor unfinished. Busoni, in a little book called *Æsthetics in Music*, says there is but one mode, the major mode.

Looking upon this question from the psychological standpoint, it is easy to affirm that for the average person the major mode is the more wholesome, since it is both more cheerful and more positive.

If you wish to learn to hear whether a

composition is written in the major or
minor mode, drill yourself on chords

and sing.

In order to read music intelligently one
has to understand the so-called relative
minor. The scale of the relative minor
begins on the sixth of the major scale.

In learning to read music you must bear
in mind the fact that the same signature
may designate either the major or its
relative minor. Also help yourself by listening intently to the first strains of any
music you hear and deciding whether it is
major or minor.

The next point to take up in connection
with the understanding of practical harmony is what is called modulation—the

changing from one key to another. It is not easy to explain this on paper.

The wisest way to approach this subject is to first hear where a tune ceases to be in one key and goes into another—that is, where its keynote changes. Take the following example:

The keynote changes from C to G at the point marked. When you have *heard* that this is so then seek to find how it changes. This involves hearing an added note to the V chord, and the five chord of the NEW scale at that. But to make it clearer here is an illustration. Suppose you want to go from the key of C into the key of G; the easiest possible modulation is to play four notes up from C—that is, C, D, E—then when you come to F, sharp it, pause and sing what you hear under it, and you have

the dominant seventh chord—that is, the dominant chord of G plus its seventh note. But it must be admitted that to do this without help is extremely difficult.

VI

MUSIC FOR CHILDREN

The education of heroes shall be gymnastics for the body and music for the soul. Begin the education with music.
—PLATO.

MOTHERHOOD is to the race what the keynote is to music. Of all women, mothers and teachers are the most important. The right attitude toward motherhood is a subject that we are just beginning to treat with any degree of intelligence and common sense.

Why, when everything depends upon bringing a better type of human being into the world, do we treat the subject of sex and children as though it were something to be ashamed of? The greatest of all teachers called the body the temple of the Holy Spirit, and yet, up to the present time, people have married and children have been born one might say carelessly, without preparation. We educate our young girls in all sorts of surface ways, give them social *savoir faire*, teaching them all sorts of superficial things, and leaving the great subject of motherhood and preparation for it, untouched.

Take the subject of music as an example. Instead of teaching a girl the beginning of music, the fundamentals, which she can in turn pass on to her children or use to enliven and harmonize the home life, we encourage her to acquire an amount of technical skill, which depletes her physically, being the wrong kind of technique, and which enables her only to play music that is over her own head, as well as the heads of most of her family and friends.

These "pieces" which she learns at such a cost of energy and time, to say nothing of her father's pocketbook, are forgotten and laid aside as soon as she marries. Ask any convention of mothers about their musical education, and you will get the same answer from 90 per cent of them. They never "seemed to get anywhere with their music, so they dropped it." Though they all wish they had kept it up for their children's sake, and husband would appreciate some simple music, too.

Girls are the future mothers of the race, and education must take that fact into consideration. Now, what can a mother do who has had the old-fashioned musical education? She can first sit down and think out the question of music for children and decide why she thinks they should have it and what results will follow in developing their lives. We need to do more real thinking to determine what things we want for our children and what the benefits are going to be.

Picture a house where there is absolutely no music, no piano, no singing, not even a phonograph or a pianola. Is there not a dead, depressed feeling about such an atmosphere? Environment is an all-important factor in the rearing of children, not merely material environment in which everything is done for the physical welfare of the child, but the spiritual environment which we may term atmosphere, abused as this word has become.

A kitchen may have a better atmosphere, and often has, than a drawing-room. Why? It is the state of mind of those who are in it. Many a mother supplies material comfort in every detail and yet starves her children of the very thing they need so much. What can music do to supply this lack? For example, picture a mother off in the country where there are no concerts, and where the village choir sings out of tune; where, if there are pianos, the ever-present popular songs are all that can be found on the racks. The children sing a hymn or two and a few songs, but music is, in the real sense, an unknown quantity. This mother can easily learn to use music for the highest and most permanent good of her children, and also her husband and friends, simply by using intelligently the limited means within her grasp. If she can read music fairly well, and most girls can, her first step should be to acquire some book of folk songs and dances (see Appendix) and some children's songs, which are simple and have constructive words.

An hour of this music just before bedtime will prove of immense benefit, for the consciousness of the child will be thoroughly harmonized and will work all through sleep in a constructive, harmonizing way. It is a scientific fact that the subconscious mind takes up the thoughts with which it is supplied, and during sleep, when the objective mind is stilled, works out those thoughts in exact likeness, producing an effect in the external life exactly similar to the cause. Therefore it is of the utmost importance that our thoughts should be happy and constructive just before we go to sleep.

An hour of good music at bedtime will so harmonize the child's consciousness that he will go to sleep happy and serene. Those thoughts will do their unfailing work of rebuilding, physically, mentally, and spiritually, all through the night, and the child will awaken in the morning in the same happy, healthy frame of mind.

Play over some of these folk dances and let the children skip around and act out what is in the dance. Musical folk games are splendid and give children a sense of rhythm. They feel that everything moves more easily when done to music, and they play together as one harmonious group. The spirit of play and joy seems quite natural.

Every mother should realize that she must supply something by which harmony is maintained. Leaving little children alone means whining, quarreling, demanding candy, toys, etc. Music is such a force for bringing people together and making them forget themselves that the older members of a family are fully as much benefited by it as the children.

We have spoken of the importance of music before the child goes to sleep. It is equally important to have it in the morning when consciousness is brought back to the waking state, to maintain that harmonious attitude throughout the day. Therefore it is of equal importance to start the day with a song or two.

The Hindus have a morning song, a song for noon, an evening song, and a song for midnight. They have songs of praise, songs of love, songs of joy, songs of peace, and many others. To them the home is a sacred temple and the parents the priest and priestess of the actual presence of God, who is acknowledged and rejoiced in with every homely event of the day. This is idealizing the real in a practical way.

It is quite easy if a mother will take the trouble to give the children the right fundamental training in music, which makes it an actually understood language to them from the very first.

A child learns to speak through speaking, to walk by walking, and to sing by singing. Experience *versus* formal knowledge is the new idea in everything. "I prefer to do rather than talk" might be the motto of the new educational teacher.

Having found within herself the laws of melody, rhythm, and harmony a mother will be able to communicate them to her children, and thus not only smooth out rough places in the daily lives of the family, but awaken in the children a real love and appreciation of music. More than that, she will teach them the right process for all study—that is, from within out. First silence, then listening, then understanding, then remembering, then singing, and finally playing.

The pleasure of music is thus made to serve a definite purpose in life, establishing a true relationship and co-ordination, and giving the children a technique by which they may live in a more practically ideal way.

But a good many mothers have no time to give to the study of music, so the work which should really be done by the mother herself must be given over to teachers, and here we must pause to say a word for and about teachers.

During the war a number of our teachers ran elevators as a patriotic service, and when the war ended they continued to do so because the salary paid an elevator operator was so much more adequate in relation to living than what they were able to earn by teaching. Everyone knows that whereas a painter, plumber, or carpenter is receiving a living wage, teachers are still getting so little that they often suffer for the lack of the necessities of life, to say nothing of the things that would aid them to become better teachers. For the study of any art by a person who aims to teach it is a long, slow, and difficult process. It requires not only health, vision, and contact with the best in the musical world, but a knowledge of general education, of the other arts, of psychology, and of child psychology in particular. To these must be added sufficient time for continued and concentrated work, and all this costs a great deal of money.

To be sure, all teachers are not single-minded, they are human, and sometimes, through chance or circumstance rather than real preference, they become music teachers from a business motive. But these are in the minority. We have found most teachers self-sacrificing and devoted to their work, pitifully lacking in the ordinary comforts of life and in the peace of mind and state of health which a little more money would give them. Even a so-called, high-priced music teacher is financially insecure. Her season is short, people are thoughtless in regard to discontinuing their lessons, and her expenses are heavier than those of other teachers. For the new teaching demands enthusiasm, and she must avoid getting into a rut. This means keeping her health, optimism, and peace of mind; it means keeping alive the artistic side of her musical life through practice, study, and contact with the world of music, and at the same time keeping her intellect awake in some big way to avoid becoming dried up. In addition, she must allow some time for her own life, for companionship, and happiness of a personal nature. So, from a purely selfish standpoint, society should consider giving teachers a comfortable living. To this remark there sometimes comes back the answer, "Too much would spoil them." A little spoiling certainly would not harm hundreds of teachers whom it has been our privilege and pleasure to know. To end this subject, here is one little incident drawn from actual life:

At the Music School Settlement we have the children of a great many workers whose trade is uncertain. Sometimes there are long periods of dullness, during which there is literally no income. When this occurs music lessons, cheap as they are and as much as they are loved and longed for, become prohibitive. At such times dozens of children drop out. During one of these periods a faculty meeting was called to ascertain whether the teachers, whose pupils had been forced to drop out, could possibly make time to visit these children and find out what probability there was of their returning. It then came out that two-thirds of these children were being privately taught *for nothing* by teachers who we well knew were driven all day long by the necessity of earning a living, not only for themselves, but in many cases for some dependent. So much for the teacher, her vital interest in her work and her self-sacrifice.

We find that five is a good age to begin the musical education of a child, though he should have had a musical environment before he was born and every day thereafter. What is meant by musical education is that a definite hour for music be set apart two or three times a week, in which some understanding person (preferably the mother) shall begin to awaken the musical consciousness in the child. It would be ideal to have a group of six children, all about the same age, assemble each day, and under the guidance of the right person play musical games, swing and walk rhythms, sing songs or sing about things just as they would naturally talk about them. We have learned through intimate contact with children that they do naturally chant or sing about everything if the teacher or mother sets the example by having songs for the simple functions of daily life.

It certainly lends romance and buoyancy to the endless washings and brushings and dressings that have to be attended to with children if we sing to them. The same philosophy holds good here as elsewhere. If you are singing with your whole being you cannot be worried, cross, angry, or really idle.

Such a class for children aims to stir up the musical consciousness of the child. The results are sometimes quite startling.

For instance, a rather awkward and apparently unmusical child, the little daughter of a well-known sculptor, suddenly began to dance so exquisitely that people asked whether she had been trained by Miss Duncan, and could not believe that she had not been specially trained.

It is difficult to describe one of these classes, and well-nigh impossible to give anyone written directions as to how to conduct one.

In one instance the principal of a big school, seeing the apparent simplicity of these classes, tried to introduce them by telling the music teachers what to do. But after a little he was surprised to discover that it was not so "easy as it looked"; it certainly is *not* so easy as it looks.

Seeing six little children dancing about to music, swinging their arms, singing songs, or playing a musical game makes some people ask, "Do you call this a *lesson?*" This makes us smile. It is such a commentary on the word "lesson." Growth is the object of all teaching; the growth of the child in consciousness to the end that

he shall really be awake in a musical sense—
if it be music that he is studying. Our
education has shown itself such a failure
in that it has caused children to be lacking
in health, peace of mind, initiative, self-
reliance, and a desire to be of service, and
needs really to be reversed from one of a
more or less mechanical process to something vital and real. The little boy who
cannot add a few figures, though he has
"finished arithmetic," and who says that
what he learned in arithmetic is the *word*
"gazinta" (goes into); the mother who has
had years of music lessons and who cannot
play a simple tune with its bass, and all the
rest, are some of its amusing results. You
can no more see the result of music lessons
in a given time than you can see a flower
when the seed has barely sprouted. No one
wants to pull up the seed and see a result,
but we think we must get results that are
concrete in the children. Children's classes
look very like play, but in order to conduct
them a teacher must be a rare person. She
is the awakener of the *spirit* of music in the
children. From this awakening springs a

definite consciousness of melody, rhythm, and harmony, which, being set up in the child, finally produces results, sometimes quite startling in artistic power and beauty, and always produces a love and a far better understanding of music than that of the average grown-up.

Singing games, with their elements of gayety, dramatic action, and social contact, make a really ideal way of beginning a children's class. Miss Hofer's book, *Singing Games for Children*, and the English singing games—in fact, those of all countries—should be used with little children. We like the "Muffin Man," "Looby Loo," "The Farmer in the Dell," and "Annie Goes to the Cabbage Patch," for the first ones, but the field is immense, and each mother or teacher can best select her own material.

Then songs for children to sing! What a field there is to be explored! In America the average child's repertoire of songs is a shocking thing. It is incredible that, knowing as we do the effect of environment upon children, we allow them to store their minds with the worst imaginable trash. To be sure we have no folk music here in this country, but we have some really beautiful songs written for children—such as the songs of childhood—of Jessie Gaynor. Then there is the folk literature of England, and France is a perfect gold mine, to say nothing of all the other countries. We use these songs, and in the class the children swing the rhythm, find the pitch, duration, pattern, and keynote of every song they sing. Transposing is easy when it is done from the listening sense. Nothing is ever done as "ear training," it is all strictly from the musical sense — that is, the creative side, sticking to the principles of melody, rhythm, and harmony as our basis.

Musical conversation, in which the teacher sings a question and the child answers it, always in the rhythm, is one of the ways of feeling and hearing the keynote. Singing a scale down to the second, pausing and letting the child complete it, is another good way; or singing a folk song and letting the child end it; or making up a tune and seeing if it really ends or needs an ending, always pausing to listen and remembering that actual performance comes last.

All these exercises can be done with the phonograph. For the swinging of rhythms there is nothing so good; the same is true in connection with stepping rhythms, skipping, and dancing. The phonograph offers a great variety of music of the very best type and is very practical where the mother has no time to devote to the learning of the necessary music, for as a teacher she has to know a great deal of rhythmic music, folk dances, and other good music, such as Bach, Beethoven, and Grieg, which she can play while the children do anything they like. This helps them to listen, to adjust their bodies to the rhythm, and, besides its musical value, has a real value in regard to health and nerves. But in this connection there is one thing that must be avoided by the teacher: never notice the fact that the child is out of rhythm. If you will emphasize the rhythm of your playing, or swing your own body in rhythm and give him time together with simple music, he will get into the swing.

We remember a child, who was in a class with six little children, who seemed hopelessly unrhythmic. His mother was quite concerned, and repeatedly complained to the teacher that he seemed never to step or dance "in time" as the other children did. The teacher, knowing better than the mother, and not having the natural impatience and vanity common to most mothers, urged her to wait until the sense of rhythm in him was really awakened. (We believe, you see, that one must be ready in order to really learn anything.) Well, one fine day, when no one was bothering over Teddy's rhythmic vagaries, he began to dance in perfect swing, and having felt the delight of it he kept on long after the other children had had enough. The teacher, seeing what had happened, played on and on, until his little fat legs nearly dropped off, but the ecstasy and satisfaction of having found it in himself made Teddy more than willing to suffer and work. This is the great point.

There is no discipline like unto *self-*discipline.

We use a blackboard continually. The children make pitch pictures, duration pictures, and anything else that helps them to let out the music they hear within themselves.

And here we must consider the element of notation. When we teach children to read their notes we do not teach them the bass and treble as two different things, neither do we separate them from melody. Rather do we seek, by training the inner sense of sight, to have the child visualize middle C in a melody like "Baby Bye" (Jessie Gaynor's "Miniature Melodies"), and to associate its picture, which looks like this,

with its sound.

We prove to them that they can see with their eyes closed—that is, see with their inner eyes, and hear with their inner ears. Children have this power of visualization (seeing with the inner eyes) strongly developed. They are able to visualize a note, for instance, that they have seen with their open eyes. Having awakened this consciousness, we draw two staffs on the board, the bass and the treble, placing middle C where it belongs—that is, on the first ledger line below the treble staff. We then have the children look at it, then close their eyes and see it. Then we erase its picture and let them draw it. After that they can go to the piano and pick it out. When this note is well fixed in their consciousness we take up in a like manner the notes above and below C in the treble and bass.

Children are full of creative ability, and little children find it easy to make their own tunes. Here are two, words and music, given by children of six:

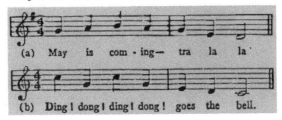

(a) May is com · ing— tra la la

(b) Ding! dong! ding! dong! goes the bell.

Music for Children

When they can make accurate pitch and duration pictures, and can read their notes, it is then well to have them write their own tunes in their own blank books, so that they may grow accustomed to writing music as well as playing it.

A class of children soon becomes quite free musically through these various simple drills, which a teacher must know how to vary to make them interesting.

The last principle to awaken is the harmonic, and we have been surprised to find that little children "hear under"—that is, hear the underlying harmonies of a tune, quite naturally. Sometimes it is enough for the teacher to begin to sing the roots of the chords underlying a song which the children are singing. Their harmonic sense will wake and they will take it up naturally. Suppose, for instance, that the children are singing, "I Had a Little Nut Tree."

The simplest harmonic setting to this tune is

$$\text{I—I—IV—I—V—I—V—I}$$

The teacher should sing the root or principal note of each chord as

After a little she can try playing the tune either on the piano or the phonograph, or she may sing it and ask the children to sing what they hear under it. Having caught their interest, it is then wisest to set about hearing the root of the I chord, or the tonic as the musicians call it. To do this play several chords, and get the children to pick out the I chord by noting its quality of rest, and *not* by telling them the name of the chord. When the I chord is made so familiar they can hear it under any simple tune you can take up the V chord. Have them note its quality of *motion* as differentiated from the I chord, and how it *always* moves toward the I chord. Do the same with the IV chord. By degrees you can give tunes that bring out a V, and later still a IV. There is absolutely no hurry in this work. The idea is musical consciousness; development, not performance. More is accomplished in the end, not only musically, but in health and character, by going slowly and insisting upon a process, which is always the same—that is, silence, listening, etc. When performance is a natural thing, and sometimes this is the case even with young children, we do not try to stop them, but we never try to speed up the playing, and never urge them to learn "a piece." The natural outcome of hearing, swinging, singing, etc., is not only playing, but composing, and a rounded musical and mental development.

Older children who have been trained in this way play little basses to folk tunes quite easily. Two children can go to the keyboard, one playing the melody and one the bass. They play it in C and they play it in G, or in any easy key, for, since it is a matter of hearing, all keys are equally simple.

This lays a foundation that has literally no end. Upon it one can either become a good listener in the true sense of the word or an artist.

Memorizing becomes an actual science, since to hear makes one sure of what to play and one loses the misery of uncertainty so well known to pianists. Analysis, through hearing, changes all of that.

The question of material is a very important one. In the children's classes every teacher adapts her material to the needs of her children.

Speaking in a general way, folk music, the Gaynor "Miniature Melodies," "The Cady Folk Tunes for Ten Fingers," and similar music is used. A teacher must be really familiar with her material. She must know whether a song is suitable for a child, whether its harmonization includes a IV chord or not, etc. The better acquainted she is with her material (she should really know it by heart) the better her teaching will be. Teaching "with a book" is never a success. In fact, freedom and creativeness are the key to the teaching of children's classes, coupled with real musicianship.

VII

PRACTICING

The reaction from personal effort is a feeling of joy and freedom.

"WHEN I was little I used to shake the hourglass to make the practice time shorter." Haven't we all done much the same thing.

"You and I could be very good friends, mother, if it were not for this horrid music," wails a little boy to his adoring parent. "Mother says, 'Now go and practice,' whenever she sees me, and so I try not to go near her," remarks another child. "I was just going to practice because I really wanted to, when the maid said, 'Your mother told me, miss, to remind you to practice,' and then I made up my mind I wouldn't." This is the reaction to be got from nagging a child or forcing a child to practice.

A doctor once ordered malted milk, and nothing but malted milk, for a child who had a severe case of whooping cough. It was a perfectly sensible order, and would have been the very best thing if the child had been the kind of child that liked malted milk and would take it. But in this case the baby refused, calling loudly for pancakes. Everyone knows that pancakes are not the proper food for a sick child of three. However, starvation seemed the alternative, and finally in the middle of the night, having carefully studied the directions of Aunt Jemima's pancake flour, the cakes were made and *fed* to her, and on them she throve. This is not a plea for feeding children on pancakes. It is merely to show that you can prescribe certain things to children, and that is one thing, but you cannot make them assimilate these things *unless they want to.* The psychology of it then is to be able to get children to want the right thing, and to do what is right for them through creating a real desire. "Desire is the soul of will." We must learn a way of getting the intense interest of children, and then they will practice without being reminded.

In the cases where we have tried this it has worked out in every instance, and every mother knows that all the preaching and forcing in the world is without avail if a child has no interest in what is to be done. "Sometimes I think with my eyes, and sometimes I think with my brains," said a fourteen-year-old girl. This is just the point; a child can actually sit on the piano stool and spend the allotted period playing the notes and all the time be thinking of skating, dolls, food, etc.

Older students do the same thing. It is the same old story of the letter and not the spirit. The result is worse than nothing, because the *love* of music is either killed entirely or the desire to learn music is given such a blow that it takes an unusual stimulus to start it up again.

It is interesting to interrogate people on this score and find out how *many* of them have had the same experience and how they regret it. It is almost always through an unwillingness to practice because of some one's nagging.

"Then you do not believe in practice," you say. You are wrong. We *do* believe in practice, and in more concentrated practice than the average child has ever dreamed of. Furthermore, we get it, but not by nagging. Let us explain. When children are taught in this newer way they are not expected to arrive at a certain given point in a given time. The teacher studies her pupils, adapts the work to them with one idea in mind: that they shall become musically conscious. But in working toward this ideal she takes into consideration the kind of child, its temperament, ability, and state of health. In adapting the work she may get a sluggish child into such a state of interest that he will surprise everyone by his devotion to practicing. A nervous child, one that works under a certain tension, and is overconscientious, has naturally to be differently treated. The music lesson is secondary to the child; the child comes first. When children are inwardly aroused—that is, when music is awakened in them, they become so interested that no one has to urge practicing. They spend hours picking out tunes and finding basses for them. Sometimes mothers call up at bedtime, begging to know what chord belongs in such and such a place, "under" such and such a tune, because Sally will not go to sleep until she finds it.

Hundreds of teachers and mothers will tell you the same story. And it is a perfectly natural thing when we remember that the one thing that we are all looking for is the Truth—and these simple fundamentals are the truth of music. Besides this, they give instant pleasure in making it possible for a child to do something himself, something that he likes and understands. To be able to pick out a tune easily is in itself a pleasure, and many a grown-up man has remarked how much he would give if he had been taught that. One of these men recently said that he had been discouraged by having to do interminable finger exercises, and made to choose between baseball and music, so he gave up music for good.

Practicing

The idea of giving the technical side of anything before having awakened a love and a desire for it seems to us to defeat the end at the beginning. To commence with finger exercises invariably means to kill the interest. Every child likes to pick out a tune, but hardly any child likes to play finger exercises. Through picking out a tune, the keynote, scale, and rhythm are naturally learned; so through the desired thing the technical part of the subject is easily learned.

And here let us say a word about another subject in regard to practicing: counting. In the first place, the object of counting is really a rhythmic one—that is, a rhythmic swing underlies time, and time is the mechanical side of rhythm. A child might count all the way through a piece and still be out of rhythm, therefore the end desired is not obtained. It is again the letter *versus* the spirit of the law. Neither does jerky counting help rhythm, rather does it hinder it. Breithaupt says: "We urgently recommend that the pupil be taught to desist from pedantically counting bar by bar;

he has too much else to do." To read the music, play with arms, hands, and fingers, and to count into the bargain are three actions which the child cannot possibly accomplish simultaneously. It is hard to get teachers to acknowledge this, but the proof of the pudding is the tasting.

It is a fallacy to think that spending a certain amount of time at the piano playing over chords, scales, and pieces is practicing. Mental vacuity is often the state accompanying these performances, so is it not better for a child to spend a few minutes in which his whole attention is taken up finding the melody that he *wants*, and perhaps finding its bass as well? When he begins to hear tunes of his own inwardly, and to pick them out on the piano, he is forever concentrated in his practice. Under these circumstances the chances are that he will devote more than the time allotted.

In one school they were obliged to lock the pianos to keep the children from practicing too much. We are always amused when people beg us to insist upon a given amount of practicing. Our advice is always to leave them alone, and in a short time you will be begging them to stop.

"My family objects to my playing hymns at midnight," laughs a mother who has taken up her music again. She enjoys knowing just what she is playing so much that she cannot leave off even at bedtime.

Children who have learned to hear inwardly eventually do a great deal of practicing *away* from the piano. That is, they learn to hear music from looking at it, just as one would read a poem. A little girl who had been taught in this way went to another city, and began to study music with a new teacher. A new folk song was put up before her, and the teacher said, "You may take this one."

The child sat quietly looking at the music. "Why don't you play it, dear?" asked the teacher. "Because I am looking it over." This child was reading the melody (mentally), getting the keynote, determining whether the folk song was written in a major or minor key, deciding about the phrasing, fingering, rhythm, and harmony before playing. It is a definite inward process, and leads to the kind of musicianship that makes music a factor in life whether one has an instrument or not, and whether one can attend a concert or not. When listening has become a perfectly definite process, when the melodic and harmonic law have become a part of you, just as walking has become automatic after one's first baby efforts, then comes a certain power. You are able to play easily in any key; you can harmonize and memorize away from the piano without effort. Our aim is to achieve this kind of musicianship, and this cannot be accomplished through a forced practicing of a certain number of hours daily.

You cannot force children to learn anything, but you can so present a thing to them that you will arouse their interest and cause them to undertake the subject of their own free will. At first they may seem uninterested, but give them a chance to act on their own impulse, have faith in the child and his unerring feeling for beauty and truth, and this will pass.

So, having aroused the child's interest in

music, leave him alone. Do not nag him to play, do not nag him to practice, and, above all, *never show him off*. Let him volunteer to play or sing, but never ask him to perform in order to impress the mother of some other child. Let music be a natural, spontaneous thing in the home, and the love of it will grow and prosper.

For the more advanced student the same general advice also holds good; but to make it more exact, and to give him a definite routine, we will give an outline of how to practice a given composition. Let us take, for example, the Bach B minor "Gavotte," arranged by Saint-Saëns, planning to study it with close attention.

Play the "Gavotte" through to get a general idea of it. If you are uncertain about what sort of dance the gavotte is, look it up. If you have not read a life of Bach, get one (Parry's is a very good one) and read it. Make sure that you are to be quiet and undisturbed when you practice, and provide yourself with a small blank book and a pencil. Play the first phrase of the "Gavotte," stop and name your key

(B minor), then play the B-minor scale and the three elementary chords of that key, I, IV, VI. In this way the key becomes subconsciously settled and this makes concentration much easier. Each phrase must be analyzed in a broad way, giving the fundamental sound, and making a rough sketch of the harmonies. Sing the melodies, then sing the root tone of the bass, and play the melody.

Rhythm and time being two distinct things, the student must decide upon the rhythmic swing of the music, and whether the accent falls on the B or the F in the theme, as:

Evidently the B is the accented note. Then practice at once pulling off the chord, with B sounding above the rest. The guide is always, of course, the ear. Concentrate on

what you want to hear and then play a
phrase slowly and decide whether you have
been able to objectify what you have heard.
The more you *listen* the better you will play.

In studying make a note of whether you
did or did not concentrate, making a cross
to stand for concentration and an "o" for
wandering. Children respond very quickly
to this way of recording concentration and
learn to hold their minds to one thing, not
only in music, but in other things. *If you
can command your thought, you can command
your life.*

Then in **your** blank book put the word
"accuracy" on another page, and after
you have thoroughly analyzed its meaning,
concentrate on playing every note *exactly
as it is written*, recording your progress.

The old way of endlessly repeating a passage has been a failure, because, while the
fingers were playing the notes more or less
accurately, the mind was wandering. If,
as scientists tell us, we made phonographic
records in our minds of our thoughts, how
much more vividly we might impress our
minds and retain the desired image if we

would take pains to be accurate and to *think* of nothing else while we did it.

We should not have to practice all day, and besides that we should be gaining in mental power and endurance with every hour of accurate concentrated work.

Next, the pedal must be carefully thought of. The clarity of the music must not be disturbed, and here *listening* is again the path to success.

It is better for the student to find his own pedaling and fingering; the marks given being only suggestive. Having gone through the composition, analyzing it, playing it accurately, marked fingering and pedaling according to your own sense of harmony and beauty, you may begin to think of how to express the message. Is this music gay or sad, and what does it say?

Some one has spoken of it as "the tallest thing ever written." It has a quality of freedom and bigness which everyone must feel, but is not half the charm of hearing different people play the charm of hearing what the composition means to them? It was Mendelssohn, was it not, who said, in objecting to program music: "How can I know what it must mean to you? A composition may mean a rose to you, and to me a cabbage."

The main thing is for the performer to *feel something*. The reason so much playing is uninteresting is that the player is not conscious of any emotion or feeling. Just try playing a simple little thing to some one and of deliberately sending out a thought, or of sending up a prayer, and you will have satisfied your audience. This is the great mental drill for each one of us. We have asked advanced pupils to tell us frankly what they thought of while they practiced or played, and the answers have varied from "purple hats," "ride on a bus," to "love of friends" and "beautiful sunsets."

There is a mystic communion in music played by the *whole self* which satisfies and helps, but this kind of music is rarely heard. Why? Because people allow their minds to wander, instead of entering into the inspiration of the composer and touching a higher, finer part of themselves and their listeners.

What Music Can Do for You

Plato says, "A false note drives away God." This is another plea for accuracy; we must be true in order to deliver the higher message. To play with "expression" means that you are absorbed in the beauty and exaltation of the music, that you have forgotten yourself, your little personal self, or "bloated nothingness," as Emerson calls it, and have entered into a higher realization of beauty and power.

There are phrases in this "Gavotte" that need special study, for instance, the octaves in the tenth measure.* Do you want them legato? If so, finger them with the fourth finger on F sharp, practicing slowly, listening intently for the nuance you want. Each time record the result, and if you once are able to play the passage legato, repeat it three times, listening, concentrating intently as you do so. Measures 18, 19, 20, and 30 will need the same kind of practice. The entire composition ought to be gone over carefully for fingering, the object being to express the musical idea

* The Saint-Saëns's transcription in B minor.

according to your ideal. If you want the passage in the fifty-sixth measure to go smoothly, try different fingerings until you discover the one that suits your hand. All hands are not alike and there can be no ironclad rule. Your *ear* is your only guide.

The next difficulty is in measure 48. Here we have the use of the third pedal. Begin by playing the bass alone from 43, and hold the F sharp in 48 with the middle pedal, releasing it at 52. Practice very thoughtfully and slowly until you have been able to do this several times. Then play the treble, finding the fingering and practice thoughtfully. Stop and play the end of 48 and 49, 50, 51, and 52, *singing* the alto voice, then play the alto and sing the soprano; in other words, study these measures until you thoroughly understand them.

Some one once asked MacDowell how *long* one must practice a certain composition. He answered, "Until you understand it." The fallacy is, that we think we understand before we really do. If a great composer spends hours and hours on a single phrase, we must be willing to spend time and thought and not to want to cover too much ground in a short time. To read through a great deal of musical literature is excellent, but when we set out to study a composition there must be no haste if there is to be accuracy and beauty.

In memorizing, make a schedule and see and hear mentally each phrase. This is slow work, but sure. The bass seems to be the main stumbling block in memorizing, therefore the student should play the treble and sing the bass of each phrase if he wants to be really sure. Perhaps the reason why so many people play better when they are alone is that they are really not sure enough of the notes of a composition to be able to concentrate on the message to be expressed when others are about. Music is the language of the spirit. When through concentration in practicing we are free from the thought of notes, fingering, pedals, etc., we can truly express our inner spiritual selves and thus give the message to those who are listening.

VIII

"Education should increase faith to such an extent that fear would be impossible."

OF the thousands who have taken music lessons for a year or more and then stopped in disgust 90 per cent will tell you that finger exercises and scales made them hate music. The young girl who begins lessons with enthusiasm is soon disillusioned by the eternal and uninteresting grind of 1, 2, 3, 4, and children get to regard music lessons as a form of punishment, invented for their special benefit. "What have you studied?" asks a new teacher. "Oh, scales, and there seems to be no end of them," answers the tearful child. We have undoubtedly put the cart before the horse, defeating the very ideal we hoped to establish. Now that everybody is agreed upon the fact that the object of the study of music is *realization*, or *consciousness*, there is a general rush toward a different and more real kind of music study. People are finding out that working for effect will always end in catastrophe. Bluffing lasts only for a while; the day of settlement is bound to come. Children are not to blame that they have found music lessons dull. Family life has lost out enormously in that young girls gave up music before they married and had children of their own.

But why have we put technique in such a wrong relation to the study of music? If we could wipe away all impressions as to what has been the way of teaching music, and start without prejudice, we might come to the following conclusions: First, that music must be felt and heard before a note is played; that music, being a language of sound, must be heard and understood in terms of sound; that no one should try to play anything until he has listened, heard, sung, and understood simple tunes followed by fundamental basses. Second,

that the technical problem is not simply
that of hands and arms, but takes in the
whole body, involving a knowledge of the
laws governing physiology and anatomy;
that tone production involves physics and
that it is in its last analysis a mental
process, based on the law of freedom through
control.

Take a child beginning to study music
(and all children should certainly be given
the chance): *what* ought to be done after
the first class lessons, which are described
in another chapter? In the first place, one
should look the child over as an individual,
for no two children are alike. There are,
of course, types, such as the phlegmatic,
vital, etc., which one might classify roughly
to begin with, adapting the treatment to the
type. For instance, almost everyone needs
to learn to relax; but a very phlegmatic
child needs just the opposite. There are
certain things we ought to think of; one
is, what will add to the health of this child,
NOT how are we going to get this child to
play a piece in two months.

A nervous child must go more slowly

than a phlegmatic one, and can be greatly helped to a more healthy condition by a teacher who understands his needs. To be sure, the whole life of a child is involved in this problem, and a music teacher cannot really supply all that is needed. She can, however, suggest a regime of right exercise and training, if it is needed, and then give the same kind of thing in the music lesson— that is, do things that will help toward establishing strength and health of body. It is better to go slowly and grow up into strong, self-reliant womanhood or manhood than to play some difficult music at an early age. People have paid too great a price for technical brilliancy. The great artist needs it; the average person does not. We need just enough technique to enable us to play simple things well—that is, the average person does. The talented people and geniuses are in a class by themselves, and we should not try merely to ape them.

A few exercises which help us to relax, gain tone, beauty, speed, and accuracy are all that are necessary. To relax is not so easy. In his immortal essay on this subject, James says, "Now do not say 'I will go right home and relax,' because you will find it less easy than you supposed."

Annie Payson Call in *Power Through Repose* gives a number of helpful suggestions about relaxation, calling attention to the way we sleep, ride, sit, etc., always screwed up in bowknots. Yvette Gilbert spoke of the mouths of Americans, and how tense their faces looked. We have all had experiences in our own lives which prove that relaxation is a help toward health and a happier life. Then there is the opposite to relaxation: a certain tension and power, which may be learned in simple ways. Last of all is speed, which is so often a limitation. Doctor Mason was a real pioneer, for he gave the real basis of technique in his *Touch and Technique*, but Matthay, Breithaupt, and, later, Schmitz, have evolved even a clearer psychological process. To have the possibility of relaxation and its opposite, to be able to plan mentally the desired speed and then get it —this is the ideal of modern technique.

The great amount of time spent on acquiring strength seems stupid, when, as Matthay puts it, a newly born baby is able to hang on a stick, holding up its own weight with its newborn fingers! There seems to be plenty of strength in them. We already *are* strong, free, flexible, and we have lightness, calmness, and speed. It is only that we need some definite means of bringing out these capacities and powers. A little technique goes a long way. First listening, then thinking, then singing, playing, and then some technical exercises to make the playing more conscious and more beautiful —this is the proper sequence.

Music is in everyone to *some* extent; but we often kill it in those whose talent is not such that they will go through endless discipline and discouragement in order to accomplish the end they have in mind.

Too much technique given too early either kills the love and desire for it or it develops a person to a high standard; this is only useful to those who are to be professional musicians. With children it is often better not to do any technical work at all for several years. With older people a little that will help limber up stiff hands and arms, combined with a definite mental control, is the necessary thing.

Technique is really an attempt to accomplish liberation of the body, and combine it with expression. From the very first the Greeks combined bodily movements with music, which seems entirely reasonable. The life of rush and hurry which we force upon our little children makes it almost impossible to carry out this idea. Children would have a better start if they could meet every day for musical and physical drills. We have frequently talked of putting this sort of thing into the school in which we are working. Plato describes such an ideal education, including speaking, poetry, rhythm, melody, harmony, bodily culture, and control. Certainly this would form a wonderful basis for a useful and happy life.

We do not want less technique in anything, we want a better, more practical technique, which will give us more power, more health, energy, and peace. One of the things that will help to bring about a practical technique is breathing. From the purely musical standpoint breathing has immense value. But we must learn to breathe. Babies breathe naturally; it is only when we begin to "educate" our children that they form habits of sluggish breathing.

Every teacher should try to study breathing herself in order to be more healthy, alive, and self-controlled mentally as well as physically. Since the war, when so much was found to depend upon a knowledge of breathing, there has been a deeper interest in this important subject. It is true that deep breathing affects the mind and that mental action affects the breathing. For instance, under the so-called newer kind of healing treatments that are now acknowledged as helpful, even by some doctors, the breathing deepens.

"Going into the silence"—that is, stilling the mind, deepens the breathing. The opposite is likewise true—that is, deep breathing helps to still the mind. Listening also stills the mind and deepens the breathing; in fact, any act of concentration will do the same thing.

Technique

The effect of continuous deep breathing on health and state of mind is easily proved. Fear in all forms, such as timidity, suspicion, doubt, worry, or depression, can be allayed by long, deep breaths.

A noted opera singer who during the war did a great deal to increase the lung capacity of officers, and therefore to increase the tone and carrying power of their orders, tells a story on himself which shows the effect of breathing on the mind. He says that up to the time of his deep study and interest in the science of breath he always recoiled from going into a manager's office, and that when he did go there he acquiesced in almost any proposal, feeling so timid and depressed that he was unconscious of the fact that he was signing himself away for twopence. Since breathing deeply and studying the effect of deep breathing he has learned to take a deep breath before entering the manager's office and he now finds himself dictating to the manager! Besides the obvious effect upon mind and body, the study of breathing can be made co-ordinate with playing. In this realm the singers have outstripped the instrumentalists and it is high time that we avail ourselves of this power which will chase away the specters of fear and forgetfulness and draw to us beauty of tone and phrase. But in going on to tone we must draw some comparisons with the old ideas of technique. Simply to get a loud tone is not the object of technique, although it would often appear so. Sometimes a pianist's playing has been described as sounding "like six pianos." But six tin cans beaten lustily will make as good a sound. We have often confused *noise* with music. "A soft voice is an excellent thing in woman," and it seems as though the average person liked a soft tone on the piano. A great virtuoso cultivates a big, resonant tone, which he needs in a place like Carnegie Hall, but children, amateurs, and lovers of music who simply want to play a little at home need not spend hours in acquiring loudness. Quality is better than quantity, and with the right physical condition, and the training which induces listening, there is very little danger of developing this fault. Pounding and banging, in the sense of loudness and brilliancy, is a curse, as many a weary man will testify.

During the war the music which we took into hospital wards had to be right in tone quality. We learned this through experience, and it is distressing to think that there were times at first when some poor, racked soul was forced to hear a voice that yelled or a pianist who pounded. There was such a demand for music that we made the mistake of accepting people on some one else's recommendation. It was the men themselves who made us realize our mistake by turning wearily to a game of solitaire. On the contrary, when some one with a beautiful mellow tone sang or played, it was difficult for the performer to get away.

Another valueless technical practice is the repetition of one figure, either scale or phrase. What would be the use of repeating words over and over if there was no connection with the mind? One could never get very far, for instance, in acting, if the words of a part were simply memorized in a parrotlike way, yet people are continually doing this in music. "Now play it twenty-five times with the right and twenty-five times with the left" is familiar to most of us. We remember a pupil who came with her arms full of exercise books— Czerny, Pishner, Hannon, Schmitt, Cramer, and Tausig. She proudly announced that she had "been through them all." "You must have a very good technique then," was the innocent rejoinder. "No, it's strange, I cannot play a thing," she replied. Is it not the fault of our entire educational system that we lay stress on getting through something in a mechanical way but do not ask ourselves whether it is worth anything practically until we have paid a fearful price in time for what has failed to yield any result?

A few vital things really understood and thought about are worth a hundred books of exercises gone through mechanically. The latter is simply a waste of time. Now that we see how these things bear on technique in music let us consider for a moment how we can achieve relaxation, proper breath control, mental control, and concentration.

Doctor Worcester, originator of the Emmanuel Movement, gave a formula for relaxation which proved of real help to people. He had them sit quietly in a comfortable chair and say (with eyes closed), "I now relax my body." Then every part of the body—head, eyes, neck, back, arms, etc., down to the tips of the toes—is told to let go. He then had them say: "I relax body and mind. I let go of all worry and fear." Such relaxation opens the consciousness for growth and permits the body to become an avenue of expression.

Concentration comes next, and this is aided by breath. So having relaxed, breathe deeply for a few minutes, then begin to play, fixing your attention on the center of your back—not on your fingers. (It is presupposed that you have memorized the notes.) Now listen to your tone and phrasing. Here breath again comes into account. Breathe in, on your out rhythmic swing, and let out your breath on the inward swing. The deeper and more rhyth-

What Music Can Do for You

mically you breathe the deeper your tone and the more rhythmic your playing.

NOTE: For fuller details see *How to Breathe Correctly*, by Edward Lankow.

IX

MUSIC FOR GROWN-UPS

If music is to prove itself the most spiritual of all the arts, it must do so by aid of the audience.
—R. H. SCHAUFFLER.

DURING the war everyone realized, more than ever before, the absolute necessity of music, and since the signing of the armistice there has been no abatement in the steady flow of people to concert halls. There now is a real love and appreciation of music in this country. The next step is to get more understanding of it. Enjoyment and benefit come from understanding, and, although we heartily sympathize with the people who object to being eternally "educated," we know that everyone is eager for a reaction that will combine pleasure with profit, provided it be not too obviously "educational." The youth of to-day assumes a lightness, a frivolity, a dislike for serious occupation that would be alarming if it were deep seated. But the root of it is unrest, coming from a decision that since present education is a failure we may as well be merry and uneducated. But prove to any person of adolescent years and scornful attitude that there is real pleasure and the possibility of growth in anything you have to offer and you will immediately get another attitude. What they want is a balance of intellect and spirit. We have said so repeatedly that music can be both emotionally satisfying and scientifically true that it may seem wearisome. It is true, nevertheless, and people have lost out so continually by being one-sided that it is about time to change.

Some of the remarks made after concerts are illuminating, in that they are an indication of the way people react to music. After a piano recital by Novaes we heard a woman remark, "Oh, isn't her shoulder work wonderful?"

After a Bauer recital of modern music- "Why did he play so many wrong notes?"

Music for Grown-ups

At a performance of Beethoven's fifth symphony—"Doesn't the horn play loud, and wasn't the conductor's hair funny?"

"Does music go up and down or cross-wise?"

"Did you see that lady in the balcony? She fainted from emotion when they played the Tschaikowsky 'Pathetique.'" (All heart and no head type.)

In his delightful book, *The Musical Amateur*, Robert Schauffler says a great many things that one could quote. He divides listeners into two classes, constructive and destructive. He speaks of the contagion of listeners, and says that even a few destructive listeners are deadly to the crowd. Harry Barnhardt, the great community-singing leader, put it in another way when he said, "Sit near the man who sings well; if you can't sing yourself you'll catch it from him." This law of contagion certainly works. The ancients used to engage great mathematicians, great historians, and great poets simply to live in the house with their children, knowing, as they did, that something of what these great minds contained would emanate to those near them.

／ So, if you want to learn to become a creative listener, select some one who hears, to go with you to concerts. Beware of the person who is musically educated but destructively critical. Choose a companion who has a right heart and is not eternally looking, as some one has put it, "for the bum note." But what is creative listening, and how shall we become creative listeners?

Schauffler describes the destructive listeners as "All head and no heart," "All heart and no head," and "No head and no heart." He tried the experiment of buying up a section of seats at symphony concerts for people who wanted to learn to listen creatively. He quotes one man who was the fortunate recipient of one of these tickets: "I shall never forget the thrill of that moment when the master's baton descended out of the tense silence, invoking the power and glory of the fifth revelation according to Beethoven, and then, as I felt something within me resounding, not only to the recreation of that music by string and reed and brazen throat, but vibrating as well to kindred resonances from the hearts about me, I suddenly saw art in a new guise. I began to be dimly conscious of music as a social power binding people by myriads of strands to all those other human beings who have tasted, or are to taste, the ecstasy of creative listening." /

But what *is* creative listening? Schauffler is a little indefinite. What we need is a little simple instruction for listeners, giving them not only the inspiring idea of what an integral part they really are of every concert, but also showing them how they can actually hear the music inwardly, and so become a very part of it. One of the simplest things for a music lover, who goes to concerts, to do is to learn *not* to look so much, but to listen.

A young girl was describing a recital by a well-known pianist whose blond hair is much admired by his feminine followers. "Oh, it was a *wonderful* recital. I can't remember what he played, but his hair looked so lovely against the blue curtain!"

Close your eyes, relax as much as you can,

stop thinking and simply *listen*. Now, to the average person who has had a year or two of music lessons and stopped in disgust, a symphony is simply, as some one has put it, "a nice noise." With eyes glued to the performers and mind wandering, people get a hazy satisfaction, a sense of ease, or a certain optimism, from hearing music, but they could easily get a deeper, more lasting, and much more fascinating effect if they decided to become musically conscious of what they were hearing. When people speak of *hearing* they are sometimes mistaken in the meaning of the term, for "to hear," as we mean it, is not the fact of not being deaf, it is the act of being inwardly aware of what is being played. There is actually an inner ear that hears and there are definite ways of learning to "hear more."

The principles spoken of before, in regard to intelligently listening to melody, rhythm, and harmony, must once more be reiterated. To close the eyes and relax enables you to concentrate upon the inner listening much better. Blind people often hear better than those who can see for this very reason. To close the eyes is simple, but to relax is different, in this day of excitement and unrest. A good thing to do is to go to the concert hall early, and deliberately plan to get into a receptive mood. When we think of how people rush from dinner to a symphony, hardly allowing time to be seated, no wonder the music means nothing but a wave of emotion or a feeling of ease. To record the event and make it at all worth the while get there early, sit quietly, and deliberately relax the body and still the mind, cultivating a mood of receptivity. Choose one thing on the program to which you are going to listen analytically and try to hear the following things: Is the music in a major or a minor key? Can you hear the keynote? Can you follow the simplest idea which we commonly call tune, a motif, or phrase? Can you feel the simple rhythmic swing of that phrase or motif? Could you make a picture in lines on your program that would enable you to store that motif in your mind, carry it home, and pick it out on the piano? Every concert should

and could yield us a harvest if we could recall
one or two tunes that would help cast out fear
and worry in times of stress, helping to build
up hope and faith in their stead. There is a
real value in being able to protect ourselves
from destructive thought by constructive
memories, such as a beautiful theme. Constructive thought leads to constructive action. Music, *stored in the mind*, is a direct
and definite means of constructive action,
which is not only a benefit to individuals,
but to homes, cities, states, and countries.

Musical education, of a simple sort, would
do more than the average mind can imagine
to reconstruct society. Everyone believes
in right thinking. Thinking motifs is right
thinking of a high and powerful order.
Given the power to hear the pitch (upward
and downward movement) of a theme, or
motif, or tune, to hear its keynote, its
rhythm, even without the harmonic setting,
you have a stored-up picture that will
arouse feelings of peace, rest, love, joy, and
altruism. These feelings can be recalled
through your power to recall to mind the
music. Through rehearsing the music with

attendant feelings, depression, discouragement, fear, anger, hate, and destructiveness of all kinds will not only be eliminated, but *replaced* by harmony, peace, and joy.

Added to the obvious strength of melody, might be harmony—that is, the fundamental bases of chords—I, IV, and V. A person who knew nothing of these chords might have to get a little help from some one who understood how to awaken what we call "hearing under"—that is, hearing the root tone of the I chord, the IV chord, and the V chord.

We are looking forward to the time when every public school will give the fundamentals of music from the standpoint of listening and living, rather than that of performance. Rich and poor need this education, and the awakening of the harmonic consciousness would do a great deal toward bringing about better social conditions. Everyone needs it—the capitalist and the cook, the day laborer and the queen. Is there anyone in any walk of life who is not looking for that realm of melody, rhythm, and harmony which he must and will finally find in himself?

X

PHONOGRAPHS AND PIANOLAS

Musical training is a more potent instrument than any other, because rhythm and harmony find their way into the inward places of the soul, on which they mightily fasten.
—PLATO.

NOW that everyone agrees that music is necessary, that every sort of person both wants and needs music, that we work better, play better, think better, and live better if there is plenty of music to decorate the atmosphere, the question naturally arises: How shall everyone get it?

It is still almost impossible for the average person to have sufficient leisure time for study. After the day's work a man needs a certain amount of absolute rest and relaxation. He needs the peace, the inspiration that music can give him; so, if he cannot play for himself, the next best thing is to have a phonograph or a pianola.

Phonographs and Pianolas

Not long ago, as we were sitting in a train, a weary brakeman passed through. Instantly we fell to discussing what kind of music he should have. He might want to play the violin or the piano; in all probability he did. For, judging from our experiences in Music School Settlements and statistics in this connection in the public schools, all kinds and conditions of men, women, and children want to play some instrument. The demand for music is enormous. Music School Settlements always have long, long waiting lists of eager applicants who, as one child said, love music, consider it a luxury, and are very happy that they can get it for twenty-five cents.

When the late Doctor Rix posted a notice to the effect that violin lessons would be given in a certain public school for fifteen cents he had seven thousand applicants. Thousands of people flock to the free concerts given on the Columbia College campus during the summer and to those given in the Metropolitan Museum of Art during the winter. It is right that there should be this free music, particularly if we want a new nation with love, beauty, and harmony as its ideal. We build cathedrals, churches, chapels, and do all we can to induce people to go to them. This is right, but why not go farther? Since God is love, love is harmony, and harmony is music, why not help people to God through free music *ad libitum*.

Music is a spiritual language that unites people of all nations. We have seen Bohemians, Rumanians, Chinese, Poles, Russians, Italians, French, Scotch, Irish, Jews, and Christians all mingling in a friendly, happy state through the influence of a settlement orchestra. For even though they may not understand English, they do understand the universal language of music.

But to return to the brakeman. He must have some music, so let us give him a phonograph, say, on the installment plan. To what constructive use can he put it? He will, in all probability, buy records and enjoy listening to them in a more or less external way, for, as some one very truly remarked, "Sometimes music is like a nice warm bath, and sometimes it's like an emotional spree."

But since the time has come to get the balance between the purely emotional side of music and the more intellectual side we must both feel and think, doing neither to the exclusion of the other. We can do both, and should do both, if we want to avoid the overemotionalism that produces inertia and immorality, as well as the over intellectuality which kills all love and joy. What can our brakeman do to achieve this happy medium?

First, he can and must be careful of the kind of records which he buys. We have learned that some music, notably an over-stimulating type of ragtime, wears out the nervous system instead of quieting and renewing its strength. Such records should be avoided. But good marches, waltzes, and folk dances with a decided rhythm to which he can pat his foot, dance, or whistle, are highly recommended. Then as his taste develops he might take some of the standard light operas, like those of Gilbert and Sullivan. To these could be added the innumerable lovely ballads which he knows and always loves. Then, if he has perhaps a little guidance, he could try stopping the instrument in the middle of a song and completing it himself, in this way awakening the musical consciousness, though without a name. If he could have more help, he might then try singing basses and altos with the instrument, thus discovering for himself the underlying harmonies of the tune.

The phonograph is also an excellent way for the children to learn good songs, as well as helping the whole family to study in an informal way with the idea of learning more. For instance, you can take a record such as Charles Harrison, singing "Mother Machree." Play the record through, having everyone listen to the tune and its ending. Let anyone who wants to, try to sing the tune to the others, and let the others judge whether he is right or wrong. Then play it over again and have everyone end on the keynote with it. Then try to hear whether it is major or minor. Having found this out, repeat it and find out what the rhythm

and time are. Then sing the end note as a
bass note like this

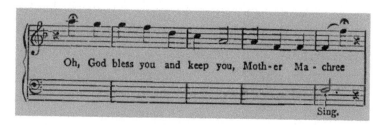

and come in with that bass note as often
as it seems to occur, like this

showing I and V chords and the basses to be sung in chorus.

If anyone can sing the root of the five chord do that. The next evening review what was done the night before. Then play one or two records, having each person simply relax to the feeling without trying to hear anything definite. Then go back to the song of the night before and review it, playing the keynote, swinging rhythm, tapping time, and "singing under."

A list of records which are adapted to this kind of study is given in the Appendix. The same thing is applicable to the pianola, only there we can take up more easily than with the phonograph the study of the terms of music, as well as its historic forms.

Where one comes across a world-famous name it is always well to read a short life of the man. This lends color to his music, gives a better understanding of the emotional side of his art, and opens up a still wider field of study.

Naturally, the course of study to be pursued through a phonograph or pianola would differ with the individual. There would be any number of people farther ahead in taste, needs, and interest than the brakeman. One person might want to prepare to listen more intelligently to a concert. Another might wish to acquaint himself with opera, while still another might only want to store his memory with beautiful songs. But in each case the only fundamental difference in procedure is the choice of records.

So through mechanical musical instruments you can obtain, if you are sufficiently persistent (for even here music requires concentration and control of mind), the fundamentals of music which will lead you to a harmonious, fuller life, and a more stable character.

XI

MUSIC AND HEALTH

The four necessities of life are food, shelter, raiment, and music.—RUSKIN.

SOME years ago a movement was started by Eva Vescelius * for healing through music. But despite the fact that marvelous results were obtained, too little attention was paid to it. The medical profession scoffed and the lay mind looked askance.

Always having believed in music as a fundamental factor in the general development of life, we felt that the development was one of significance and determined to test its possibilities.

We gathered groups together and had some one play, while those of the group

* *Music and Health*, by Eva Vescelius. To be obtained at The League for the Larger Life, 227 West Seventy-second Street, New York City.

recorded the effect upon themselves by
jotting down a word or two, such as
courage and hope, as the effect produced
by Chopin Prelude No. 1; peace and
harmony, that of Beethoven Op. 31, No. 3
Minuetto, etc.

Musical meditation was another experiment—that is, improvising on the piano to
certain words. Taking such a phrase as
"infinite goodness," some one played softly
and rhythmically to the group for about
five minutes. Soon the music had its
effect upon both player and listeners.
Through such experiments we found that
music was one of the greatest helps in
accomplishing constructive meditation.

But up to that time we had only experi-
mented, then one day came an opportunity
to prove the results. A young woman was
dying. Her baby had died at birth a few
weeks previously, and since that time the
mother had steadily failed. The doctor had
just left her room saying emphatically that
there was no hope and to give her anything
she wanted.

She looked up at her agonized husband

and said: "Music. I want music. I know that will cure me." Fantastic as the idea seemed to him, he could do nothing but hasten to give her the thing she craved. So they brought her to us, motoring many miles. The nurse in attendance looked askance on what seemed to her a foolhardy and useless errand.

The first day old familiar tunes and some of the Chopin that she had always loved, especially the "F-sharp Major Nocturne," were played softly to her. Her body relaxed under the soothing influence, her nerves became less tense, her breathing deeper and more rhythmical, increasing the circulation. That night she slept. With the shutting of the senses to the outside world the harmonic reaction brought about by the music continued its work of healing all through the night.

The next day she was visibly stronger, so the music played was of a gay and rather forceful character—Grieg's "Wedding Day" and some folk dances. A flush of color and hope came to the faded cheek. Her mother, nurse, and husband all admitted the rapid change, and the patient herself announced that she was going to live, which she did.

Over and over again men and women who have not rested for weeks fall quietly to sleep under the influence of musical therapy. Those who have insufferable worries are able to unbosom themselves, headaches disappear, depression is relieved, and severe fevers are assuaged. And why not? Musical healing is not merely an emotional thing which takes a patient's mind off his troubles for the time being. It is a scientific fact and its benefits are lasting.

All sound is vibration and communicates itself by waves. Physics tells us that "When a tightly stretched violin string is set in transverse vibration by plucking or bowing it, a sound is heard, and it can be seen by the blurred appearance of the string that it is in rapid vibratory motion. As the vibration dies away the sound becomes fainter and fainter and ultimately ceases. If the vibration is suddenly stopped by touching the string, the sound at once ceases." Wave motion travels out from the source or body which produces it—in the case of music, this is the instrument—to the surrounding atmosphere. The sensation of sound therefore is produced by the wave motion from the source of sound on the ear drum.

This phenomenon of physiology is generally admitted and understood at its face value, and as we go deeper into it we see that through the sense of hearing the plexes of nerves in the human body catch the vibrations sent out from the source of sound and vibrate sympathetically with them, just as the mute strings of an instrument will respond to waves of sound set in motion by the plucking of the strings on another instrument in the same room.

As everything in the universe is in vibration, thought likewise travels in waves. With these scientific facts before us we see that when one relaxes and listens to music, the sound waves and the thought waves combine to carry their vibratory message, producing a similar effect upon the nervous system of the body, which is the most finely and delicately constructed wiring system known. It is not difficult to see, therefore, that the proper selection of music plays a very large part in musical healing.

If the patient is depressed and the nerves are unstrung the Gavotte from "Iphigenia," or something similar, will raise the vibrations until the delicate wiring of the body is in tune. If the nerves are taut and tight, almost to the snapping point, a selection should be chosen which will relax and loosen them until they are vibrating in sympathy with the music. They are then ready to carry the message of health, hope, faith, and courage to all parts of the body. Breathing becomes normal and rhythmic, awakening the circulation, and the spirit of harmony pulses through the whole human organism.

Indeed, thought carries so perfectly through this medium that it is not only possible but easy to communicate ideas. We once played the Bach "Gavotte in B Minor" (Saint-Saëns) to a man who was unusually sensitive but not in the least a musician. He gave the following perfect analysis of our thought. "In the beginning, the word joy was the theme; in the middle, something happened." The fact of the matter being that we wanted to use the third pedal, and in the effort to find it the thread of the thought was lost.

Constructive thinking to music is the consciousness of the sound itself plus a mental and a spiritual consciousness. If people who play are thinking of their fingers, their notes, or of their own performance the audience registers that. Perfection of technique and note is necessary, but the rest must also be there, else the real inspiration and help which can come from music is lacking.

Music makes anything go. It makes a peace meeting more peaceful, it intensifies the spirit of courage in soldiers, it makes drunkards drink more, it seduces, it uplifts, it stimulates workers, it soothes and it heals. We are to decide its use, destructive or constructive. Nothing is wholly good and nothing is wholly bad; it is the use we make of it which determines its effect.

Since the war doctors have begun to

admit the wonderful help of music, not only in cheering the depressed, but in actual healing. One of the doctors in a war hospital not only approved greatly of music in the wards, but brought with him from his own hospital in the West an experience that is worth citing. This man was a lover of music and a thorough believer in its therapeutic value. He proved to his own satisfaction and that of his colleagues that by using certain records on the phonograph he was able to reduce the amount of discomfort, as well as the quantity of the anæsthetic about to be administered to patients who were being prepared for operations. He had music played to them as they went under the anæsthetic, and again as they were emerging from its effects.

Doctor Peterson, the famous neurologist, showed us a little Swiss music box which he had had made for his patients suffering from insomnia, believing that it would help them to sleep. He smilingly remarked that its only drawback was that it ran down, and for that reason, if for no other, a human being with an instrument was preferable.

The war precipitated the practical application of music to health, giving us many opportunities to try out its efficacy. It also gave us the opportunity of proving that the *mind* of the person who is either singing or playing has a great deal to do with the effect of the music upon the listener. In the hospital wards men instantly felt the difference between a person who simply performed music and one who meditated while playing.

The following case came to our notice when we went out to one of the hospitals for men who were unable to go "over" on account of illness. It was our third visit there, and since there were so many wards that we could not cover them all we went to those which we had not visited the week before. A fine-looking young fellow, clad in a dressing gown, kept coming out of one of the wards, beckoning to us and then disappearing. At last we decided to go and find out what he was so persistently calling for. His eyes glistened as he said, "If you only knew what this music has meant to me you certainly would come." We returned to his ward, where we played and sang, and he told us this story: He was from the Middle West and had only been married a few months when a telegram came, saying that his wife had died suddenly. He went all to pieces. "They took me to the nut ward," he said, "and I didn't think I would ever come out. Then one day you people came in with the music. I never can tell you what a sudden feeling of restoration and health came to me when the lady played on the violin." ("The Swan," by Saint-Saëns was the piece played.) "I knew I was well," he continued, "and could hardly wait for the doctor to confirm it and send me over. I realized that I must forget my personal sorrows for the sake of my country, and I did. Here I am going to be discharged to-morrow, and going over next week." His blue eyes shone as he said: "There's something about the music you play that we all feel. It's different from the rest; seems to go right to the spot and gives us courage."

What Music Can Do for You

The people who played that day had consciously ministered, both mentally and musically, to these men. Musical meditation is much more powerful than the performance of music by some one whose thoughts are wandering and whose mind is not concentrated.

A nun in one of our suburban hospitals played her patients to sleep instead of giving them the prescribed narcotics. The doctor, skeptical at first, was glad enough to get such good results without the disagreeable reaction from drugs. In all hospitals the day should begin with music. Music should, as some one has aptly put it, decorate the atmosphere continually and keep us all in touch with the realm of harmony in ourselves. It should be a bridge between heaven and earth, but we have been misusing it. In one of Tolstoy's books he complains of a girl who insisted upon practicing or, rather, banging one passage of the Liszt "II Rhapsody" over and over. He also writes in the *Kreutzer Sonata* of the sensual effect of music. Both times he is justified in what he says, for in many cases we have misused music.

Music and Health

It is one thing for great artists to practice hours and hours on the difficult compositions of Schumann, Liszt, Bach, and others. They have a right to reproduce these masterpieces for those who can understand and appreciate them, it being their life work; but for the average person it is futile and vain, and worse than a waste of time. If the ordinary person would only learn to hear and understand some beautiful and simple music and to play with a mellow tone, instead of whacking the piano, we would have the full benefit of music, physically and spiritually.

The ordinary practicing of music is destructive to the nervous system. Look at the physical wrecks who have returned from Europe, or even from some conservatories in this country. We are mad to allow our children to destroy themselves in this way. I have a case in mind which clearly illustrates this point.

Two women met and went into ecstasies over a foreign teacher with whom their respective son and daughter had been studying. At the end of the conversation one mother asked the other, "Where is your son now?" "In a sanitarium," answered the first woman. "And where is your daughter?" "She is dead," the other replied, sadly.

One very rainy night a young crippled girl, who had sacrificed a great deal to get down to the settlement for a normal class, finding herself the only member of the class who had braved the storm, asked the teacher to play for her. The latter knew how ill she was, and also knew how to meditate when she played. She played many things, always with some constructive thought in her mind. After the hour was over the girl stood up, and thanked her, saying: "There is something different in the way you play. I cannot make it out, but I had a bad headache when I came in and now it is gone. Besides that, I had quarreled with my stepfather, and now I am at peace with him inwardly and shall go home and make it objectively true."

Now we know that music will be more than doubled in its spiritualizing effect if the mind of the player is fixed upon some constructive or soothing or awakening thought. It is this that we call musical meditation.

During the last few years all of us have realized that our hectic living is wrong—rushing madly from one thing to another, asking questions and not stopping long enough to hear the answer, dragging our children from one lesson to another, and then surfeiting them with all sorts of artificial amusements. All of this seems like a game invented to prevent anyone from pausing to think. Have we really come to this, that our state of mind is too undesirable to be allowed a moment's chance in which to register?

Various new kinds of religion, such as Christian Science, Unity, New Thought, Divine Science, Bahaism, and some of the Eastern philosophies, are asking people to keep still, at least for a few moments each day. The contention is that in doing this the inner voice will speak, and health, peace of mind, and control of environment will be the outcome. A great many people will tell you of practical instances in which they have spent a profitable half hour in silence, or how they have become convinced of just what course to pursue, thus working out a hard problem victoriously. Orthodox religious people will say, "But we have been told from the days of Moses and David to 'Be still and know that I am God.'" Yes, but they have not been still, nor have they known that they were God. The answer of a certain clergyman rather exemplifies this attitude. On being told of what a New Thought noon hour of silence had done for one of his parishioners he said: "Yes, it is true that meditation is good for the soul. I'm sorry I am so busy that I never have time for it."

A little book called *The Practice of the Presence of God*," written by a sixteenth-century monk, tells of how the author lived every moment of his very practical and useful life in the consciousness of the Divine Presence, being in a continual state of meditation, even while he was peeling potatoes in the kitchen.

Musical meditation is a combination of this attitude of mind and music. Dr. James

Porter Mills was the first person to make this happy combination — music and thought. At his meetings he gave drills in concentration, to music. The first time it was done the wonderful sense of rest and the ease with which one could hold a thought made us realize its power.⟩

Last winter we had the pleasure of speaking to the congregation of Doctor Guthrie, whose famous old church, St. Marks-in-the-Bowery, is so well known for the practical nature of its spiritual life. In speaking of musical therapy, musical meditation was naturally touched upon. Doctor Guthrie insisted upon holding a meditation then and there. We took the words, "Infinite Goodness," improvised softly to these words, the four hundred people, cultivated men and women, joining in the silent thought to music. After the meeting a number of people, especially men, came up and spoke enthusiastically of the rest that it had given them.

For musical meditation, a program could be made such as this: for insomnia—"Peace, Perfect Peace"; for depression, in connection with some serious illness that may look hopeless—"The Joy of the Lord Is Your Strength," or just Joy or Power or Love; for headache—Harmony and Love. There are two ways of directing this musical meditation, one is to improvise to the words; the other, to choose some very good melody, such as Rubinstein's Romance in E flat, Chopin's F-sharp Nocturne, or the C Major Prelude No. 1, which are all good for this purpose, using appropriate words, such as have been mentioned, while you play.

Learn to pick out a tune, and to find the chords that go with it; you can then add to this some words of health, joy, peace, or aspiration and see how it will link you to the heavenly realm within yourself and make you physically better. If you have a phonograph, listen to that in a more conscious way, using different records for different purposes, as Chanson d'Inde for abstraction into higher realms, or a Strauss waltz for the joy of life.

If you go to a concert and have learned to hear the fundamentals of Melody,

Music and Health

Rhythm, and Harmony, associate with this music some words of the master poets, or quotations from the great scriptures, such as the New Testament, the Bhagavid Gita, or the Koran, and to you will surely come more harmony of mind and body, and from you will radiate more health and love to those about you.

XII

THE PHILOSOPHY OF MUSIC

Music is a moral law. It gives a soul to the universe, wings to the mind, flight to the imagination, a charm to sadness, gayety and life to everything else. It is the essence of order and leads to all that is good, just, and beautiful— of which it is the invisible but nevertheless dazzling, passionate, and external form.—PLATO.

WE began with the idea of finding a means of bringing out of ourselves more joy, more health, more love, and more happiness, through the inner realization of music. The concluding thought is, that the remedy for all ills is education. Real education develops energy, power, and, best of all, faith. It develops so much faith that there is no room for fear. Faith in anything is a tremendous asset, but faith in one's own inner connection with the source of all power and truth changes everything for the better. Nothing will succeed without enthusiasm, fervor, energy, and faith. Let us go back and trace the steps which finally lead to this faith-consciousness.

We rise or fall through our senses. Our training has been so very superficial and unconnected with life that we must virtually be re-educated.

In the teaching of music we have looked for a superficial effect, rather than for real training. The sense of hearing is naturally to be trained through the study of music. Music study also involves the senses of sight and touch. These senses linked up and in an active state give us what we call feeling. To really listen is much more difficult than we realize, because our bodies are not in perfect condition, and we are accustomed to such scattered mental processes. To still the mind means a powerful control—and who has it?

Listening, then, or, better yet, silence, is really the first step in *hearing*. Sound, color, and form are the three sides of everything in the material universe, and the natural universe is our means of contacting the invisible universe, the deeper consciousness, the self, or God. If we will but take the material given us and use it we will really develop. The brain is said to be capable of 90 per cent more development than we give it. Our hearing is practically unawakened, even in the everyday sense, because we do not listen. Some one comes from a distance to ask a question; while you are answering it he is thinking of something else or asking another question. No one listens. Listening involves concentration, and who can concentrate?

Music stands in a much closer connection with pure sensation than any of the other arts, for they depict images of external objects, whereas in music the sensation of the tone is in itself the material of the art. This sensation is only to be had through concentrated listening.

Through the very simple drills given in the preceding chapters one can learn to concentrate and to listen. Music is, one might say, organized sound. Its laws are simple. It is a combination of beauty and order which everyone loves and needs. It is for everyone, not only for the talented few. It is for everyone as a means of development, and is not merely a means of performing upon some instrument. It is a form of consciousness to be attained through individual effort with the help of a few definite exercises. The banker needs it, so do the cook, the brakeman, and the philosopher. It is no respecter of persons, but free to all who will take the trouble to work it out in the simple way which leads us to a fuller life.

We want to learn to be in tune with higher vibrations, because we realize that we shall have more joy, more health, more happiness. To attain this is both possible and practical. If we are, as most of us believe, gods in the making, the process is from a lower to a higher vibration. The writer has not enough technical knowledge of physics to speak deeply of the science of sound, but reasoning it out from a common-sense survey of the subject it appears to be in this wise:

A pig likes to be scratched on his back-low rate of vibration; a cat likes to have her fur stroked—again low rate of vibration;

the ear receives the impressions of rumbling wagons—a little higher, but still a low rate of vibration; the wind howls, the sea rages, water splashes—a little higher rate. Then comes a rhythmic sound, a drum or something like it, in which there is regularity. Then the sound begins to move, up or down, and to have a particular resting place—keynote. Then another element is heard, making a foundation for the melody and rhythm, until at last we have a complete thing—a combination of three elements of beauty, which we call music.

We all know that a temporary sense of rest, joy, or pleasure comes from hearing music even without understanding it. This can be multiplied a thousandfold, giving the faith-consciouoeness before spoken of, if one can *really* hear and so enter into the world of music. Nature lovers know a feeling of unutterable joy caused by ocean, sunset, trees, and scenes of natural beauty. The same state can be obtained through music when it can be photographed or registered on the brain and rehearsed in the absence of musical instruments. But the great question is, how shall everyone be given a chance to enter into this inner world of music? Symbolically, music stands for the harmonizing principle in life, and practically it so works out if we are willing to be very·simple about it. Listening has been known down the ages as a means of spiritual development. Learning *really* to listen is what brings us in touch with ourselves, and through this inner contact we get the answer to our problems. The scriptures of all countries lay great stress on stillness, and every great philosopher has given days and nights to silent meditation. It is all quite a simple and not at all a supernatural, mysterious thing, this relaxing and listening. Many a business man has attained success through what he calls a "hunch." In other words, he retires to his office and waits until he feels or hears a definite guidance in regard to his special problem.

What better technique could anyone have than the power to retire to an inner sanctuary within himself, there to obtain the right answer to any problem? "Singing under," as we call singing the roots of chords, has developed this power in many a child, so that they have had the capacity to still their minds and really listen to guidance which has saved their lives and brought them happiness. To "hear under" brings a sense of security, which in turn develops faith—faith in that inner kingdom of harmony which, as one of our great teachers has put it, "makes every man his own best companion."

The fact, then, that in music law and order reign is proved without question. We have seen that there is a melodic law unfailing in its exactness. We have seen faith restored by the recognition of this one fact—faith in an unseen Power which is orderly and justly working out everything with mathematical precision. (If you send out a thought of hate, fear, or worry you will receive the same. If, on the other hand, you send out one of love, faith, and hope the same will be returned.)

If we are really musically conscious, music brings us to a feeling of harmony within and without which at once becomes

religious. It is better to be able to pick
out some little melody with one finger and
really hear it than to play a Beethoven
sonata in an external way. A tune is
essentially a spiritual thing. We can neither
see it nor *touch* it. Listening inwardly
and learning step by step how to retain
the consciousness of this tune, so that we
may in time of stress rehearse it, protects
us from feelings and thoughts that are
destructive. No one really enjoys being
destructive, either outwardly or inwardly.
The price paid is far too great. Imagine,
then, a form of general education by which
each person became convinced that within
himself was the "meeting place with God,"
harmony and order, plus the answer to any
and every problem. Would it not be a
form of universal religion with practical
results?

Little children are ahead of adults in this
respect; help them to retain it by connecting their musical education through
songs, musical games, and little tunes of
their own making. Grown people, who
have to work, should have had this training

in school. Everyone should be given these fundamentals of listening as a regular part of his education.

Concentration of mind, so much talked about and so rarely attained, is one of the results of intelligent listening. Concentration is consecration. One of the great mystics has said that all we can ever give to God is attention. Listening trains the mind to pay attention. Schools, in fact every type of life—domestic, industrial, and professional—are full of people who have too little power of concentration. It is the obvious reason for failure in any undertaking, be it business or religion. But interest must precede this much-desired concentration, and music, studied from within, proves itself to be intensely interesting, one might say fascinating.

Connect music with words and you get one of two things, a song or a chant. The repetition of any constructive idea is helpful, and, when music is added, it becomes doubly so. Chanting has been, and still is, a part of all ritual, and rightly so. It is simply singing constructive words in a simple measured way. "Music makes anything go. Chant your heart's desire, and it will come to pass."

Modern chanting, or chanting to the tunes known by people of to-day, is a strong help, both in its healing power and in character-building. Fine characters will live fine, helpful lives. "As a man thinketh, so is he." For the religious life of to-day we prescribe some gay singing on arising in the morning. Control depression and laziness by singing while you bathe, exercise, and dress.

The power of the word is mighty. A child will laugh at a bump if you teach him to say "funny" when he falls down. So it is with us all. What we say about it, and what we sing about it, determines its effect for good or evil upon us. Some of the New Thought, Christian Science, Unity, etc., people have absolutely made themselves over by persistent constructive chanting. A woman, in some articles on success, ordered her pupil to say "joy" sixty times every day. It seemed ridiculous, but at the end of the sixty times her depression had fled! And, laugh as we may, the proof is in the result. Now chant something joyous over and over and see the effect. The dancing and chanting followers of Eastern cults had a grain of truth in them which did powerfully affect their lives.

Repetition of the same tune to given words with improvised basses that vary a little will induce sleep in some racked person whose eyelids have not closed in many an hour. Mothers are wise when they croon to their babes. In the hospitals we have had wonderful experiences, both with our soldiers and children. A place cannot maintain gloom where there is music plus a right mental attitude. People cast gloom over whole companies if they are inwardly depressed or perturbed. But they can also change a gloomy group into a joyous one through a mental attitude of harmony and cheerfulness. Mental integrity is what we need in this world of ours, people in tune with themselves who are thinking in a constructive way about the "other fellow."

Music is in a sense a religion, in that it teaches us to practice what every bible has preached—*love*. Love and harmony are synonymous. We look and long for the day when this power to retire to an inner state of harmony has been awakened in every living individual. Ignorance is the only sin. Light comes through stillness and listening. Music is really an invisible world, the world of beauty and of order, which we can find within ourselves. Music, we repeat, has been regarded too much as an accomplishment and too little as a means of development. To urge a child to learn to play "pieces" before he really hears inwardly is to spoil a spiritual realization for him and blunt his power of solving the problems of life. Children, when they are very small, are full of faith. Music, heard inwardly through listening, certifies faith in a wonderful way. Therefore we should let the children develop slowly and truly by hearing before they play.

If every child in our schools, public and private, could only have this early training in listening and understanding the law of order and harmony of sound to be found within themselves, this would be a far better world in which to live. Some one has said that knowledge is "the arctic zone of the soul," and this is indeed true of music. To try to get an effect—that is, to perform, before we are inwardly conscious, is starting in the wrong way. Our education, essentially in music, has always seemed to dodge the beginning. If we want what the mystics call "God consciousness" we must be willing to begin. Impatience is one of our very worst faults. No parent in the Settlement ever wanted to see the word "beginner" on his child's music; he wanted "concert." Everyone of us is guilty of this in some degree, and it is, absolutely, death to progress.

All the letters of the alphabet tacked on to a name will not make a really fine person; so all the external equipment musically possible will not bring you in actual touch with the inner harmonic world which *is* music. Music *is* religion in the sense of its being a form of consciousness common to all who have let go of the outside and listened.

To be master of environment is to be master of life. Music gives the necessary development for this attainment. We only register what we actually let in. We can change conditions by symbolically dipping every inharmony into the harmonic world within ourselves and thus transmuting it into harmony. A young girl once did this by clinging persistently to a little tune while chaos reigned around her. We can always dwell mentally in a world of our own, and music is a means given us by which we may turn failure into victory, and chaos into calm.

Listening forces us to look within, to seek and know ourselves. The inner world is the real world. "Be still and know that I am God" in terms of to-day is, "Still your body, relax, and listen." You will not only hear the end of the tune and the fundamental chords, but you will learn that by stilling your mind you will be able to get the right answer to your problems. Follow this inner listening with action and you have a perfectly balanced philosophic basis for both music and life.

From within out, this is the process, this is education, this is the road to health and happiness.

What Music Can Do for You

Harmony shows us that there is always a resolution to a dissonance—that is, a solution to every problem, and if we will listen, we can hear it. A good foundation brings good returns. A foundation laid within will unfailingly bring returns on the objective plane. A harmonic state of mind is sure to be externalized in outer conditions of harmony. "Love in search of a word," is Sydney Lanier's definition of music. This language of love is in a sense a silent language in that stillness is the first requisite for hearing. A person who lives harmoniously is inwardly conscious of an unqualified faith and happiness based upon a state of consciousness. If each person were at home with himself he would have neither time nor desire to defame his neighbor. Through his own harmony he would *affect* and *infect* others. Through our mental habits we either add to or subtract from the general harmony of the world. Give to everyone a little training in listening and he automatically becomes a part of the ocean of faith, love, and harmony which is finally to enfold us all as one great family.

Made in USA - Kendallville, IN
1101562_9781938772542
05.08.2020 1001